THE OBJECTIVE LEADER

THE OBJECTIVE LEADER

HOW TO LEVERAGE THE POWER OF SEEING THINGS AS THEY ARE

ELIZABETH R. THORNTON

palgrave
macmillan

First published in 2015 by
PALGRAVE MACMILLAN® TRADE
in the United States—a division of St. Martin's Press LLC,
175 Fifth Avenue, New York, NY 10010.

Palgrave® and Macmillan® are registered trademarks in the United States,
the United Kingdom, Europe and other countries.

ISBN: 978–1–137–27989–7

Library of Congress Cataloging-in-Publication Data

Thornton, Elizabeth R., 1958–
    The objective leader : how to leverage the power of seeing things as they
are / Elizabeth R. Thornton.
        pages cm
    ISBN 978–1–137–27989–7 (alk. paper)
    1. Leadership. 2. Success in business. I. Title.

HD57.7.T46 2015
658.4′092—dc23   2014025714

Design by Newgen Knowledge Works (P) Ltd., Chennai, India.

First edition: February 2015

10 9 8 7 6 5 4 3 2 1

Printed in the United States of America.

To my wonderful family:
Mom, Dad, Leslie, Hugh, and Weaver, who lovingly helped
shape who I am

To my dearest friends:
Susan, Kailash, Terry, and Sharon, who supported me along the way

And most profoundly...

To my teacher, most trusted advisor, and strongest advocate:
Swami Dayananda Saraswati, who inspired me to
learn, teach, and live...objectivity

CONTENTS

Part V   THE OBJECTIVE ENTREPRENEUR

INTRODUCTION

Have you ever overreacted to a situation, taken something personally when it was not really meant that way, misinterpreted the tone of an e-mail? Of course, we all have. We all respond subjectively to everything we experience. Our challenge is that we perceive through our senses— a person, situation, or event—and in an instant, we project our mental models (i.e., the lens through which we see our world) onto that perception, which often results in cognitive errors, meaning we interpret, judge, and respond incorrectly. It is the nature of the mind and the nature of being human. We are constantly appraising our environment, and if we are honest with ourselves, we have to admit we often get it wrong. We just don't see things as they really are. Although this subjectivity impacts all aspects of our lives, it can be especially destructive in business.

Demands on today's managers are greater than ever before. Massive amounts of data are available to analyze. Changes in market forces are less predictable and more complex. Yet business leaders are expected to make better decisions, faster, and implement those decisions on accelerated timelines. So when the pressure to perform intensifies, managers tend to draw on their past experiences and underlying assumptions, which clouds their ability to see things as they are and respond to changing dynamics in an unbiased or objective manner. The consequences can be significant: Deadlines are missed, emerging market opportunities are undercapitalized, relationships with suppliers are misjudged and overvalued; business models are not adapted to changing market conditions, strategic alliances are compromised, customers are lost, internal relationships become strained, reputations suffer, promotional opportunities diminish, and in many cases, health and well-being suffer.

Today, effective leadership is less about subject matter expertise. A key distinction between good leaders and great leaders is the ability to reduce cognitive errors and increase objectivity when it counts. Objectivity is defined as the ability to recognize and accept things as they are without projecting our mental models; objectivity means responding thoughtfully, deliberately, and effectively to the people, situations, and circumstances in our lives. It's also the ability to question the underlying assumptions we make when judging situations, making decisions, and taking action. Objectivity is the ability to understand another person's point of view and incorporate diverse perspectives into problem solving and decision making.

In *The Objective Leader*, I share my hard-won knowledge to help you become a great leader. Specifically, this book will help you reduce the tendency to overreact to situations, take things personally, jump to conclusions, and judge people unfairly. It will help you evaluate situations more clearly, make better decisions, execute more strategically, develop more productive relationships, and collaborate more effectively. It will help you distinguish between what is actionable and what is only in your mind. *The Objective Leader* will help you identify unproductive or ineffective mental models that are getting in your way and create winning mental models to help you get things done.

My greatest hope is that this book will help you reframe the way you see yourself. It will help you strengthen your self-concept so that you are less dependent on external validation and more grounded in an acceptance of, and appreciation for, your unique gifts and talents. My wish is that at the end of this book you will embrace the fact that your power comes from being who you truly are. You will know that being yourself is the best way to create new opportunities and possibilities for your life.

In Part I, "The Case for Seeing Things as They Are," I present Chapter 1, which tells the story of how my own lack of objectivity cost me a million dollars. Although this is a true story, I have used fictitious names to protect the privacy of others involved. This experience underscores—very painfully, for me!—the dangers of subjectivity and the need for objectivity. As I tell the story, you will see Reality Checks along the way that highlight key questions to think about. While I use other real examples and anecdotes that are also protected for privacy, I will reflect back on these Reality Checks to answer the questions posed and share with you how I might have responded more objectively. I will also highlight Lessons Learned to illuminate key takeaways from my experience along the way. In Part II, "You Can't Be Mad at Your Mind," my goal is to present an understanding and acceptance of our natural tendency to be subjective. Chapter 2 introduces the key definitions of subjectivity and objectivity and establishes that we are all inherently subjective. I have presented a few extreme examples of subjectivity to illustrate how quick and easy it is to overreact and respond in ways we often regret. These examples will help clarify and provide the context for learning how to be more objective.

It is important for you to understand that you are not alone. In Chapter 2 I also share the results of research that shows how often we tend to overreact, take things personally, and judge people quickly and unfairly. We will then set expectations for what you will be able to achieve after reading this book. You will clearly understand what it means to increase your objectivity and how to get there.

The first step is to understand how we relate to the world. Chapter 3 explores the subject-object relationship and how your mind and brain work together as an integrated system to help you navigate your world. You will learn the neuroscientific basis for why we are all inherently subjective and why it is natural for us to be so. We will also discuss drivers of our inherent subjectivity: mental models, thoughts, fears, and intuition, which all influence how we respond to our environment. And most importantly, you will learn that we all have the capacity to be more objective because of our brain's neuroplasticity—its ability to change with new information.

Once you have a good handle on what is happening in your brain when you make cognitive errors as well as the capacity of the brain to change, Part III, "Framework for Objective Leadership," focuses on making it actionable. Chapter 4 will discuss a framework for increasing objectivity, including the objective decision-making process. In Chapter 5, we will talk about increasing our objectivity under pressure, which requires interrupting our automatic responses based on current wiring and instead responding more consciously. In Chapter 6, we will talk about identifying and transforming limiting and unproductive mental models; this will help you rewire your neural net and reframe your world.

Finally, to help connect the dots, we'll take a deeper dive into the power of seeing things as they are. In Part IV, "The Objective Leader," we examine objectivity as a core competency for effective leadership. In Chapter 7 we will focus on seeing people as they are in order to manage diverse teams and create inclusive environments. In this chapter you will learn how unconscious biases are constructed and how they can inhibit a leader's ability to be objective. It shows you step by step how objective leaders transform their biases so that they can treat people fairly and incorporate diverse perspectives into problem solving and decision making. In Chapter 8 we will evaluate the effectiveness of your mental models to produce the leadership results you are seeking. Specifically, we will examine how well your mental models are helping you create collaborative team dynamics. The chapter provides a real case study of a seasoned executive who learned that there was a gap between the mental models she had about team effectiveness and the assumptions of her team. The chapter walks you through her process of understanding the team members' mental models and then leading the team in creating more effective ways to communicate and collaborate. Further, this chapter discusses the challenge of organizational mental models undermining team effectiveness and overall productivity. The chapter describes another real situation in which the senior leader guided his team in developing and supporting a new mental model that would enhance communications between the team members in order to improve patient care. And finally, building on the reported challenges of former Microsoft CEO Steve Ballmer in leading change, this chapter concludes with a framework for objective leadership in managing large-scale change initiatives.

Part V, "The Objective Entrepreneur," is for those of you who are aspiring entrepreneurs and are considering the possibility of being your own boss one day. Chapter 9 helps you objectively evaluate entrepreneurship as a career path. One of the key takeaways from my personal story is how important it is to balance passion with objectivity. Is it possible to be both passionate and objective? How can you leverage the power of seeing things as they are to create and sustain a successful venture? The goal of this chapter is to empower you with the latest thinking about the entrepreneurship process and how successful entrepreneurs really think and act. The chapter starts by acknowledging—and debunking—common myths about entrepreneurship. The chapter cites key research to provide you with the knowledge to transform limiting or unproductive mental models about the entrepreneurial process. Then we review the five common mental models that were identified in Chapter 6 and discuss how these unproductive mental models can be destructive to entrepreneurs. Once you understand the entrepreneurial process and the mental models of successful entrepreneurs, the goal of Chapter 10 is to empower you with the tools to create a sustainable venture. This chapter presents a new framework: The Objective Entrepreneur's Business Model Map, which walks you through the key components of the business model and provide tips and new ways of thinking to ensure that you are engaging the entrepreneurial process with greater objectivity. The book concludes with final thoughts in Chapter 11.

To get the most out of this book—to increase your effectiveness and transform your life—requires an open mind and a commitment to self-reflection. As you read, I want you to ask yourself the following questions: Can I validate that statement with my own experience? Can I relate to what is being said with my existing knowledge, my direct experience or observation? It is in the wake of knowledge and understanding that true transformation takes place.

After much self-reflection, it turns out that losing a million dollars, while excruciating at the time, turned out to be the best thing that ever happened to me. Through such a disorienting event, I learned to be more objective about myself and the people, circumstances, and events in my life. I am now happier and more effective than I have ever been.

This is what happened...

Part I

THE CASE FOR SEEING THINGS AS THEY ARE

Chapter 1

LACK OF OBJECTIVITY COST ME A MILLION DOLLARS

There I was, "Miss American Express." My entire definition of myself was centered on what I did. And I made sure I did it well. It was 1986; I was 28 years old and the director of sales for American Express, responsible for $1.5 billion in revenue, eight states, and six direct reports. American Express had selected me for the Executive MBA program at New York University's Stern School of Business. I was making more money than I knew what to do with. I had a company car and a condo overlooking Manhattan. I even had a personal shopper to maintain my successful image.

Confident, young, cute, and totally naive, I left American Express and moved to the Washington, DC, area to be closer to family. Armed with an MBA and a track record of getting great jobs, I was sure that advancing my career in a new city would be easy enough. But then months went by, and I could not find a job. The unemployment rate in DC at that time was 11 percent, but of course I thought I'd be the exception. I decided to start a sales and marketing consulting company called Bethington Enterprises. I was sure I could attract clients immediately. After all, I had trained at American Express, and I was very good at selling and relationship management.

> Reality Check: Was I being objective? Is there a trade-off between positive thinking, optimism, and objectivity?

The clients, however, did not come. So I decided to be proactive. The headlines at the time were all about a former governor of Arkansas who had just been elected president of the United States. I decided to go down to the Presidential Inaugural Committee Headquarters and see what I could do. I walked in the door and said, "Hello, my name is Elizabeth Thornton, I have an MBA, and I would like to help in any way I can."

A Secret Service agent, a very big guy with a gun, said, "Just sit over there and wait with the other volunteers, someone should be coming along shortly...And whatever you do, don't go beyond those glass doors over there."

I sat down and greeted the other people, but I kept my eye on those glass doors. My mother had always told me that I could do anything I put my mind to. She had never let my siblings, me, or any other young person she came across shy away from something we wanted. So, as soon as the big guy with the gun looked away, I dashed through those forbidden doors. I acted as though I belonged there, greeting people as they walked by. That day I ended up going through another set of glass doors embossed with the words "Presidential Inaugural Committee (PIC) Executive Offices, Co-Chairs Harry Thomason and Ron Brown." I didn't know this at the time, but Harry Thomason was a Hollywood producer who directed and produced hit TV shows like *Designing Women* and *Evening Shade*. Ron

Brown, who died tragically along with 34 others in a 1996 plane crash in Croatia, was the soon-to-be US Secretary of Commerce.

I introduced myself to a woman named Bobby, who appeared to be working with Harry, and asked if I could help her with anything. She took me into her office and found something for me to do. I can't remember what it was, but Bobby and I hit it off. She introduced me to Harry, and within one week I became the executive assistant to the co-chair of President Clinton's 1993 inauguration. Wanting to make an impact, I used a simple Excel spreadsheet and designed a critical-path system for managing all 30-plus inaugural events. That system was later discussed in an interview on the TV show *48 Hours*.

I ended up doing similar work as a volunteer at the White House for the first 100 days of the Clinton administration. I even turned down an offer to work in the West Wing for Alexis Herman, assistant to the president for the Office of Public Liaison. Why, you may ask? Because the salary was only a third of what I had made at American Express, and my responsibilities would have been largely administrative. Go figure.

THE NEXT BIG HEADLINE

Still uncertain about whether I'd done the right thing by turning down a job in the White House, I began working as a marketing consultant for an IT company as I searched for the next big headline. Since I was a little girl, I have always wanted to help people and make a difference in the world. Working in the corporate arena, I felt disconnected from that part of myself. So perhaps unsurprisingly, the headline that caught my attention was Nelson Mandela.

In September 1993, I watched a CBS segment entitled "End of Apartheid." They announced that the United States, Canada, and other nations were lifting most of the remaining sanctions against South Africa and were welcoming it back into the international community. This was part of the process that had begun three years earlier, when President F. W. de Klerk had announced Nelson Mandela's release from prison, thereby signaling the start of the slow dismantling of the apartheid system. Apartheid was established by Afrikaners, an ethnic group of Dutch immigrants that currently represents approximately 7 to 11 percent of the South African population. Although the Afrikaners were the minority ethnic group in the country, the Afrikaner National Party gained control of the government in 1948 and established laws to restrict the ability of other ethnic groups to participate in government. Different races were strictly segregated. Whites had access to much better housing, education, employment, transportation, and medical care. Blacks could not vote and had no representation in government. In 1992 a whites-only referendum had approved the reform process, and on April 27, 1994, the first democratic elections would be held in South Africa, with people of all races able to vote. The Government of National Unity was formed, with Nelson Mandela as president and de Klerk and Thabo Mbeki as deputy presidents.

All eyes were on South Africa. American companies were thinking about expanding their operations there, and some South African companies were exploring the possibility of entering the North American market for the first time since 1964. As an African American woman, this moved me greatly, as it did many people. What happened next was truly exhilarating.

Reality Check: Is headline searching an objective approach to the entrepreneurial process of opportunity identification and evaluation?

In late 1993, my older brother was among the hundreds of businesspeople heading to South Africa to explore product opportunities. The company he worked for had just transferred him and his family from Chicago to Johannesburg. My brother had always been health conscious; he rarely drank soda, he preferred juice. He had started drinking a South African fruit juice that he thought was delicious. An entrepreneur by nature, he tracked down the company and arranged to meet with its director of international markets. His name was Pieter.

In the meeting my brother told Pieter, "Now that sanctions have been removed, your juice could be really big in North America. I have a sister who owns a marketing consultant company in the United States. Why don't you see what she can do?" Pieter agreed. Apparently, identifying small companies to "test the waters" was the company's process for gaining access to new markets. They had done this in 64 other countries and planned to do the same with the US market. Soon, they would send products to a small firm in Boston to test the New England market and to a company in Atlanta to test Chicago and Atlanta. They would send products to me to test the markets in DC, Maryland, Virginia, and Pennsylvania.

My brother called to tell me the South Africa Fruit Juice Company (SAFJC) had just sent me 240 pounds of juice. Unable to visualize how much this was, I asked, "Will 240 pounds of juice fit in my car?"

He said, "No, probably not."

Not long after that, I received a call from the port of Baltimore informing me that I had a shipment of juice. I rented a van and drove to the airport to pick it up. It was disgusting. The juice was packaged in an aseptic container (much like many milk products are packaged today), and a few of the boxes had broken open during shipment. Bugs and flies were everywhere. Also somewhat disturbing was the fact that I couldn't read the label on the package. It was written in Afrikaans, which was the official language of South Africa during apartheid. The only English words were "Product of South Africa."

Thanks, brother, I thought to myself as I tried to figure out some way to get 240 pounds of leaky juice into my rented van.

When I got home, I threw out the spoiled containers and put some of the unspoiled juice into the refrigerator. The next day, I sat down and tasted the peach juice. Wow! It really *was* good. I poured myself another glass. I was so excited. I looked outside and it was a beautiful day, the kind of day when you think everything is possible. My mind was spinning with the following thoughts: *I can't believe how great this product is. There is nothing like it in the States. My brother was right.* And then all of sudden, I had what felt like an epiphany. I actually said out loud to myself, "I am going to do something big with this juice. I am going to earn the distribution rights for the entire US market and give 10 percent of my pretax profits back to South Africa to help Mandela transform the country."

In that moment, with the sun shining, providing what felt like clarity and insight, I decided that I wanted to establish a center to help educate and empower the black population, newly freed from the shackles of apartheid. For nearly 50 years, the apartheid government had segregated living areas, education, medical care, beaches, and other public services, and provided black people with services inferior to those of whites. Finally, here was my opportunity to help people and make a real impact on the world. I was going to help save South Africa. I said to myself, "What if I could actually meet Mandela, wouldn't that be amazing?" Instead of "Miss American Express," I instantly became the "Fruit Juice Lady." With this new identity, for the first time in a long time I felt excited about getting up in the morning. I had a giddy feeling, the same feeling I had as a little girl when I knew I could be helpful or after realizing I had been. I now had a new purpose, a new reason for being!

Reality Check: Are you seeing a pattern here? Is it possible to be objective when you are predominantly defined by the job you have or the role you play?

THE FRUIT JUICE LADY

The Food and Drug Administration had just enacted the Nutrition Labeling and Education Act of 1990, which required all products to display nutrition information on the label. I decided that unless the product was tested by an independent lab for quality and nutrition, I wouldn't touch it. I was concerned that even though the juice was distributed in 64 countries, it might not be safe by US standards. Did South Africa have an FDA? How could I ensure the safety of the product? I was able to leverage my contacts at the White House, who put me in touch with Dr. Simpson, a high-level executive at the FDA, to guide me through the process. Dr. Simpson suggested an independent lab in Maryland and also put me in touch with US Customs agents to help me understand the requirements for importing a fruit juice into the United States, specifically into the port of Baltimore.

My colleagues also facilitated a meeting with the highest-ranking South African diplomat to the United States (I'll call him The Diplomat), the first black person to hold that position. I told The Diplomat about my relationship with the SAFJC and my commitment to give 10 percent of my pretax profits back to South Africa. He was very impressed with this and felt it could serve as a model for other companies to do business in South Africa. When things got rolling, he said, he would help me establish a charitable trust in South Africa to set up the training and empowerment center.

Two months later, my company, Bethington Enterprises, presented a proposal to the SAFJC to become the consultant for US distribution. My goal was to eventually become the preferred distributor by adding undeniable and indispensable value to the company. The proposal was accepted, and in April 1994 I flew to South Africa to meet with Pieter, the director of international markets. He arranged for me to stay in a beautiful hotel in Cape Town and also took me sightseeing. We drove to Cape Point, a popular tourist site where the Indian and Atlantic oceans meet. We found it easy to talk to one another, and during the drive Pieter told me about how much he traveled, being responsible for the distribution of the fruit juice in 64 countries. He expressed his excitement about being able to enter the US market after so many years. He committed to doing anything he could to help me get the product ready for US distribution.

Later, over a cup of tea back at the hotel, Pieter signed the consulting agreement and pledged to wire 50 percent of the contract fee upfront. It was an exciting moment. Before he left he took the trouble to meet with the concierge to arrange for transportation for me back to the airport the next day. On the flight back, I remember thinking about how nice he was, and how well he accommodated me. For me this was a good sign, a sign of a potentially good relationship.

I returned to the United States; the SAFJC contract fee had hit my account and I immediately began the arduous task of identifying and complying with all the FDA requirements for juice. I contracted with the recommended lab to conduct pesticide testing as well as microbiological and authenticity testing and to measure the vitamin and mineral content for the entire 24-flavor product line. This process took about nine months. During this time, I did an extensive analysis of the beverage industry to determine if there was a gap in the market; whether industry forces were favorable, and if so, the key success factors; and, finally, if and how the product could sustain a competitive advantage.

I learned that it was clearly a tough, capital-intensive business, and there were formidable challenges in securing and maintaining shelf space in supermarkets. On the other hand, the product was 100 percent pure fruit juice in a variety of unique flavors (not just orange, grape, and apple), and it satisfied a compelling need in the emerging health-conscious consumer market. There was a clear gap in the fruit juice segment of the beverage industry, which made the overall opportunity attractive to me. (Besides, I was going to save South Africa!)

In early January 1995, the lab results came in. I called Dr. Simpson at the FDA and asked him to review all the documents. He reviewed all the materials, the laboratory results, and nutrition labels for the entire line and gave me his informal approval that I had met all the requirements for US distribution. I immediately faxed a copy of the labels to the SAFJC.

I have to admit that at that moment, I was very proud of myself. After all, I hadn't known anything about fruit juice before this, and now I knew about vitamin C dissipation rates and how many bug parts are allowed per 250 milliliters of juice. I was an overnight expert—definitely the Fruit Juice Lady, and I loved it.

Reality Check: Can you be objective about what you are doing if you have pride in what you are doing?

PROOF OF CONCEPT

Throughout the nine-month FDA compliance process, I had developed a close relationship with Pieter. He was coming to the United States for the Fancy Food Show at the Javits Center in New York, so we arranged for a meeting of the three US distributors in New York. In that meeting, I handed Pieter a complete binder—with a red bow on top for effect—of the hard copy test results, and a nutrition label for each of the 24 products. I was elated when he expressed his appreciation and acknowledged that the SAFJC would not have access to the most sought-after market in the world were it not for the efforts of Bethington Enterprises. My strategy—and all my effort—was clearly working.

In July 1995, the product arrived at the port of Baltimore. It was the first official US entry of the SAFJC juice from South Africa. The other two US agents also received product that month. The race had now begun. My understanding at the time was that the SAFJC planned to penetrate the US market slowly. It was going to monitor the progress of the three initial US agents for the first year, and then assign the distribution rights for additional states based upon sales performance.

I was not sure about the motivations of the other agents. My goal was to leverage my relationships with Pieter, as well as with The Diplomat and his family, and position myself as the leader. As my mother always said to me when I was growing up, "The worst thing that can happen is that it doesn't work out, but there is no possibility of it working out if you don't try your best." I was determined to give it all I had.

I shifted into high gear. I converted my home into an office and, with the income from my marketing consulting job, set up my infrastructure pretty quickly. Without prior knowledge or experience in the beverage industry, I was surprised that so many people were so helpful. My plan was to get the fruit juice into a high-end natural food store, similar to Whole Foods, in the mid-Atlantic region. I knew that if this upscale store, with its health-conscious clientele, were to sell the juice, I would be able to attract beverage brokers, gain access to wholesalers and supermarket distributors, and achieve mainstream distribution.

I called the store and got an appointment with Michael, the beverage buyer. Michael loved the juice and said he would give it a try. He would permit me to do in-store demos or product sampling in eight stores around the region on a Saturday, and if the product did well, he would put it on the shelves in all 26 stores.

This was a make-or-break moment for me. I had to establish proof of concept. I had to prove that customers would buy the product. What could I do to make sure the product sold out in all eight stores? I thought about this question for days, and finally came up with an idea. Instead of employing ordinary, everyday volunteers to conduct the product sampling, for that one Saturday in August 1995, I hired drop-dead gorgeous male and female models from New York. Stunningly attractive men and women stood behind the tables in all eight stores, handing out samples of the fruit juices and encouraging people to buy. Frankly, I still feel a little uneasy about this tactic, but it worked.

We sold out. I now had proof of concept upon which to build a business. Well established at the high-end natural food store, I could now attract investors and raise capital.

Reality Check: Was hiring New York models to conduct my in-store demos an objective test of consumer response to the fruit juice?

Over the next several months, I secured a beverage broker—the top broker in the area—and was assigned a team of three experts to support the launch of the product. Beverage brokers are companies that specialize in helping importers and distributors establish and maintain distribution in specific markets. They became my partners, teaching me the business and telling me how much money I would need to raise in order to successfully launch a product in my four states. With their input, I put together a comprehensive business plan, which included an official US launch at The Diplomat's office in Washington, DC, and a local TV advertising campaign. I sent it to the SAFJC for their approval. I insisted that before implementing my plan, I had to have a firm commitment—a signed five-year distribution agreement with the company for my four states. I felt that by now I'd proved my mettle. Indeed, Pieter readily agreed to a five-year exclusive distribution agreement and to my business plan.

The date was set for January 31, 1996. Pieter agreed to fly to DC for the event, and we planned to go to my attorney's office beforehand to sign the distribution agreement. I felt proud and important to have organized the official US launch of what The Diplomat called "the first major consumer South African product into the United States...in a post-sanction era." It would also be a fundraising event for me.

Everything was on the line. By this point, I had raised $100,000 to start up the venture through the Small Business Association (SBA) small business loan program based on my consulting income. But after inventory costs, in-store promotional support at the natural food store chain, and the 50 percent down payment on a 30-second commercial to be previewed at the official launch event, I was just about out of cash.

But now that I had proof of concept in 26 natural food store locations, my financing strategy was to invite high–net worth individuals and everyone else I could think of to the event so that they too could participate in history being made. Representatives from the White House were coming because of the new Gore-Mbeki initiative, known as the US–South Africa Bilateral Commission. My beverage broker and a very large supermarket distributor were going to be there, and they had invited buyers from all the major supermarket chains. These buyers could take the fruit juice into 750 additional locations if we could commit to local TV advertising with their store name tagged in each commercial and to in-store promotional support. I knew I had to raise $525,000 to support these stores, purchase inventory, and handle my overhead for the next six months. I was very nervous, and I couldn't seem to get rid of a nagging feeling, a knot in my stomach.

> Reality Check: Do you ever get a knot in your stomach? Do you know what it means? To increase your objectivity requires being aware of such sensations and understanding what they mean.

A SUCCESSFUL LAUNCH

The big day arrived, and Pieter and I went to my attorney's office, as planned, to sign the distribution agreement. I was elated and also relieved. At that time, I was the only agent with a signed distribution agreement. My strategy was working. Clearly, I was the leader.

By the time we arrived at The Diplomat's home for the launch event, the knot in my stomach was beginning to dissolve. I escorted Pieter to the second floor, where the event would take place. I made sure he was comfortable with a glass of wine and then excused myself to find The Diplomat so I could share my good news. He was upstairs in his private residence. I walked confidently up the stairs with the newly executed distribution agreement tucked in my briefcase. I sat down with The Diplomat and showed him the agreement.

He said, "You have done such a great job. I will do anything I can to support you, but you have to be careful." My heart sank. Could he be serious? I asked him what he meant, and he said that a piece of paper would not protect me, that as a result of apartheid some Afrikaners are very biased and can be tough business partners.

Perhaps he was exaggerating, I thought. I could surely handle whatever came my way. I was not that naive. I had already encountered my share of bias and toughness growing up. When I was in the fourth grade, my twin sister and I had integrated a small private Quaker school in the suburbs of Philadelphia. It had caused quite a stir when a student called my twin sister the "N" word. We got past it. I ended up president of the class through tenth grade, then president of the student council. By the time we'd graduated, my twin and I had totally transformed the school. We had Smokey Robinson playing at our graduation. Clearly, everyone had gotten over it.

Since then, I'd walked around with a mental model that I could overcome bias by just being undeniably competent. This mental model had been validated during my time at American Express in the early 1980s. I had set up an appointment to meet with a banker in Wichita, Kansas. Apparently, I didn't sound black over the phone because when I got there the banker said, "When did American Express start hiring black people? I do not do business with black people." The security guard then escorted me out of the building.

After I'd recovered from the shock and hurt, I decided that I would never tell my manager about what the banker had said and done. I would not request a transfer; I would never use my race as an excuse for failure. So, I kept calling the banker. I focused on making the business case for why he needed my product in his bank. My case was compelling, and finally he'd agreed to see me to talk about the product. After enduring racist jokes at every meeting, I finally won his business. It was an $11 million account, and with that I was promoted and got the heck out of Kansas.

So I became eternally convinced that if I could make the case—if I could add real, quantifiable value—then I could overcome any bias. How much worse could things be in South Africa? I figured I would do what had worked in the past: make myself so valuable that they would get past any issues they had with me. Besides, how could I quit now? Downstairs were friends and colleagues from Smith Barney, Shearson Lehman, and many other high–net worth individuals. My dearest friend, Ted, was also there. Ted was my peer mentor at Georgetown, and, unlike so many mentors I've heard about, he took the job seriously. I was a freshman and he was a junior, and for two years he always checked in on me, gave me advice, and was a strong source of support. Although we lost touch after college, I had heard that he was a managing partner of a leading New York investment bank. Since he always believed in me, I wanted him to come to the event, check things out, and give me his perspective. More importantly, I was hoping he could help me raise the money I needed. In addition to the people from the White House, people from the US State Department and US Department of Commerce were also there to support what was hoped to be the beginning of strong United States–South Africa business relations. And of course Michael, the beverage manager from the natural food store chain; my new brokers; and potential distributors were all sipping South African fruit juice downstairs. My entire family was also there, supporting me all the way.

Before going downstairs, The Diplomat reassured me that he would do his best to support me, and that he was very proud of all I had done.

Reality Check: What would you do at this point? My options were to (1) quit while I was ahead in fear that things might get tough; (2) pull back, take it slow, find out more, and wait to see what happens next; or (3) leverage the momentum and forge ahead. I forged ahead. Was I seeing things clearly? Was I being objective?

We walked downstairs together, and then we officially launched the South African fruit juice into the United States. The event was a great success.

Ted was very impressed with the launch event and the relationships we had established, and he pledged his support to help me raise the $525,000. Armed with the support of The Diplomat, Ted set up meetings for me with several high–net worth individuals who had experience in the beverage industry. The plan was that if a certain former president of a US beverage company personally invested in Bethington Enterprises, then Ted and

18 of his colleagues, also managing partners of the prominent New York investment bank, would follow. These extraordinarily accomplished men were all accredited investors, meaning they had a net worth of $1 million or more and an annual salary of $200,000 or more.

I met with the former US beverage company president in a conference room overlooking the Boston cityscape. After tasting the juice and hearing my presentation, he reached into his inside jacket pocket and handed me a check for $100,000. I almost fell out of my chair. I had never received a check with so many zeros. I was honored to have this powerful person's trust and support. More importantly, it was obvious that he trusted Ted.

All my ducks seemed to be lining up. The universe was with me. Naturally, I took all this as confirmation of my initial vision that first morning I'd tasted the peach juice. I was going to make a lot of money for myself and all these other fine people, and in the process I would be helping the people in post-apartheid South Africa. After meetings with several of the other partners, I raised the $525,000 needed to leverage the opportunity. Thanks to Ted, we were officially in business.

A PROBLEM BREWING

The business model was relatively simple. Bethington Enterprises would fax a written purchase order to the SAFJC, and the company would fax written confirmation within ten days. The SAFJC would fill our orders within eight weeks, which included the six weeks shipping time, allowing us to receive the product with a minimum of 11 months' shelf life. We then had to pay the company on an open account 90 days later. Bethington Enterprises had to fill orders from its US customers within five days. With freight charges, customs broker fees, and warehousing costs—including storage, pick-pack, and drayage—our gross margin was 27 percent.

Things were moving along nicely. Our operational processes were in place. Every Monday, my accountant, my operations person, my beverage broker, and I would meet for breakfast to discuss the rate of product movement in stores, new orders from existing customers, and the status of potential new customers. It was critical that we achieve sales of 2.5 cases per week per store in order to maintain our position on the shelves at our mainstream supermarket chains. We had to implement our marketing campaign quickly to keep our product on the shelves. We were focused on maintaining sales, and our brokers were focused on expanding sales. In May 1996, we presented a proposal to the SAFJC to expand fruit juice distribution into 26,000 stores. I also continued to act as the consultant for US distribution during this time and handled any regulatory issues that popped up with the FDA or US Customs. My relationship with SAFJC was strong, evidenced by Pieter and me traveling to Zimbabwe to speak at a conference representing SAFJC and touting the new US–South Africa business relationship.

The first sign of trouble came when things started getting a little sloppy on the shipments. We had to invest in shrink-wrap technology to repackage product that was improperly packaged, coded, and shipped by the SAFJC. Our stores would accept the product only if it was packaged in a certain way. I accepted this as a normal part of doing business, perhaps because it was around this time that we started to make a very small profit.

We decided to take the first steps to honor our commitment to give 10 percent of pretax profits to South Africa. Delighted to hear this, The Diplomat introduced me to his brother, who lived in Cape Town. The Diplomat's brother helped facilitate a meeting with a South African attorney to write up an agreement for a charitable trust and arranged for a real estate agent to start looking for property to house the training and empowerment center.

Meanwhile, the other two US distributors and I met periodically, at Pieter's request. The relationships started off cordial and supportive but became increasingly strained over time. The greatest point of contention was product marketing. Bethington Enterprises was getting advice from the beverage broker to position the juice as a premium product, with limited couponing and aggressive in-store demos. Everyone else wanted to do aggressive couponing. We never resolved this, so the marketing support for the product was different depending on the US agent. Given my passion to save South Africa, I must admit that I was not particularly open to other points of view.

> Reality Check: Can you be objective and collaborate effectively when you feel so certain about your position that you are not able to consider other points of view?

Suddenly, at one of our meetings, there were two new players, Afrikaners from an import company based out of Canada. Apparently, they had the exclusive distribution rights for all of Canada. Pieter, SAFJC's director of international markets, wanted all of us to work together. It was very clear that these newcomers did not agree with my marketing strategy. They seemed to have long-standing relationships and connections with the SAFJC. They referenced people I had never heard of. As a result, I started to doubt my leadership position and my strong relationship with the company. I was so glad to have my signed distribution agreement. But even so, these new guys were definitely a red flag. It was possible that they were indeed tough business partners as The Diplomat suggested. The knot in my stomach came back.

Despite these minor disruptions, by June 1996 we were in 750 stores. We were running a $300,000 advertising campaign, doing in-store demonstrations (normal ones, not with New York models), but another, potentially larger, problem was brewing.

Orders were taking four to seven months to get to the United States rather than the eight weeks as stipulated in the distribution agreement, and consequently we were receiving product with a shelf life of only seven to eight months rather than the minimum 11 months we needed. To complicate matters, Bethington Enterprises needed sufficient inventory on hand to meet demand, but we had no sales data yet for forecasting sales. To prevent running out of inventory, we had to order enough product for six months of anticipated sales, but it was impossible to sell through six months of inventory within the 90-day timeframe to meet the payment requirement. A break-even analysis indicated that Bethington Enterprises would have to sell five cases per week per store to sell through six months of inventory and pay the payable due within the 90-day period. Sales were averaging 2.5 cases per week, which was enough to stay in the stores but not enough to pay the SAFJC in 90 days. As a result, that June Bethington Enterprises owed the SAFJC $225,000 and had no cash.

I was in constant contact with Pieter and assured him that we would raise the money, but the shipment delays were causing an inventory and cash flow problem for us. Needless to say, all of my attention shifted toward raising the money. Ted, on behalf of all the investors, picked up the phone and called Pieter, inquiring about the overdue balance and how the SAFJC would treat it. Pieter informed Ted that Bethington Enterprises was the SAFJC's best-performing American distributor, accounting for 75 percent of US sales and doing the best marketing job, and that they wouldn't do anything to harm us.

Reality Check: Given the SAFJC's behavior to date, was it objectively reasonable to take them at their word that they would do nothing to harm Bethington Enterprises? Was I being objective about the strength of my relationship with my supplier?

THE FAX

Based on his discussion with Pieter, Ted helped us raise $75,000 in less than one month, which we promptly paid to the SAFJC. Also during this time, anticipating that the four- to seven-month turnaround on orders could continue being a problem, we offered the SAFJC a solution to mitigate our risk. We presented them with a central distribution plan for the eastern United States. We identified sources for the fruit purees and an aseptic packager who could manufacture the product locally. This would benefit Bethington Enterprises and the other distributors as well. Also in July, we received a positive written response to our proposal to expand into 26,000 stores and were given additional distribution rights for three states.

In August, we incurred additional costs for repackaging product that was improperly packaged, coded, and shipped by the SAFJC. Meanwhile, sales were still going well in the stores.

By September, we increased distribution from 750 stores to 1,200 stores. We also sent the SAFJC an additional $60,000, and we had begun discussions with sources of SBA debt financing for a $750,000 line of credit. At this point we only owed the SAFJC $80,000, and we were continuing to get orders for more product. We felt that we would be okay.

Somewhat confident that we could increase sales with the new stores and the new states, we were still very concerned about the shipments. Ted and I both spoke to The Diplomat to bring him up to date on what was happening. He thought it made sense to write a letter to his friend, the executive chairman of the holding company that owned the SAFJC. In the letter he called me an extraordinarily talented African American businesswoman. He said that he was truly proud of my project and would be writing it up as a model for the South African president for how big and medium-sized businesses can work together in the United States and South Africa to meet our greater social challenges.

I was grateful for The Diplomat's letter. He described me in such glowing terms and made my business efforts sound so important to the new South Africa that I was sure Bethington Enterprises would prevail.

On the evening of October 21, 1996, I walked downstairs to the basement of my house to do some laundry. I heard a beeping noise. It was the fax machine, which was out of paper. I found a roll of paper to install, and out came a letter from the SAFJC stating that my distribution agreement was terminated because of nonpayment, and that my last order was never shipped.

I fell to my knees. I was out of business!

Naturally, the first person I called the next morning was The Diplomat. He was appalled. He immediately handwrote and faxed a note to the executive chairman expressing his outrage that I was given no warning, that SAFJC's conduct was legally improper and that once I introduced the product into the country with the support of his office, the SAFJC issued a distribution agreement to other ex–South Africans. He requested that

SAFJC meet with me to work things out and expressed his disappoint-ment that their actions were "too much like yesterday's society."

The Diplomat suggested I get on a plane to South Africa. He called ahead and set up meetings for me with ministers in the new South African government. When I contacted Ted and told him about this latest devel-opment, he was angry that the SAFJC had not honored its assurance, made in July, not to harm Bethington Enterprises. Ted did not want me to go to South Africa empty-handed, so with the support of the investors as guarantors, we were able to obtain a tentative approval, which would be put in writing and signed by the president of a bank in Philadelphia, for $750,000 in financing, contingent upon a demonstrably strong relation-ship with the supplier, the SAFJC.

Armed with a track record of sales and distribution in over 1,200 stores, representing more than 75 percent of the US market, the capacity to pay, and with The Diplomat paving the way for me, I got on a plane on Tuesday, October 29—exactly one week after receiving the termination letter—and flew to South Africa to fight for my business. I was scared to death. At this point I knew I was in way over my head. Throughout the entire 19-hour flight, my mind was spinning with all kinds of scenarios, none of them good.

The next day, Wednesday, October 30, was a busy one. The Diplomat had set up back-to-back meetings for me. My first meeting was with a South African government minister, the equivalent of our secretary of commerce, and his staff. After I had presented the chronology of events and the current situation, the government minister said, "This is not about the $80,000 that you owe the SAFJC. It is about the old way of doing things and the new black South African government."

I didn't quite understand what he meant, but I felt supported when the government minister delegated one of his directors to attend the meeting with the SAFJC. He also instructed a special advisor to help me establish a relationship with a South African company owned by black South Africans.

My next meeting was at Stellenbosch University with Edgar, a good friend of The Diplomat who happened to be a previous board member and current consultant with the SAFJC. We met over lunch. Edgar was very warm and open, and he was visibly angered by the situation. He said that the SAFJC's behavior was sinister. I'll never forget what he said next: "You know, Elizabeth, you have two reputations here in South Africa. The first is that you are a savvy business woman, and the second is that you are a bitch."

I thought to myself, *I like the business savvy part, but what was the bitch thing about?* "People know that you are trying to set up an empowerment center," Edgar continued, "and they don't like that at all."

Back in the States, where excitement for the end of apartheid was palpable, helping to support South Africa had seemed relatively straight-forward and easy. Now that the plan was coming together and people were beginning to hear about my intentions, it was clearly not for some of the folks on the ground in South Africa.

By the end of that lunch, Edgar offered to help. He said he would attend the meeting between the SAFJC and me. He committed to calling the chairman of the SAFJC at home to find out what was really happening. As we shook hands goodbye, he said, "Keep the pressure on. Don't give up!"

Later the same day, The Diplomat put me in touch with the legal advisor to one of the highest officials of the new South African government. Her name was Jacoline. She referred me to a South African attorney. Jacoline also said that she would write a letter on behalf of the high government official to send to the chairman of the SAFJC a letter expressing his concern and requesting a justification for their behavior.

Meanwhile, back on the home front, there was good news: the $500,000 term loan portion of the financing deal had been approved. As I went to bed that night, I was exhausted and jet-lagged. Despite the alliances I made that day, I was still very fearful.

Reality Check: Can you be objective and make good judgments when you are fearful? What was I afraid of at this point: losing my business, my reputation, or my self-concept?

The next day, Thursday, October 31, I met with the South African attorney who agreed to represent me and accompany me to all the SAFJC meetings. *So far, so good,* I thought. I returned to my hotel to find a fax from The Diplomat. It was a copy of the letter he had received from Willem, the managing director of the SAFJC and Pieter's boss, which stated that he understood The Diplomat's concerns and would meet with me on Tuesday, November 5, "in an endeavor to resolve the issue."

Handwritten by The Diplomat on the faxed copy was an encouraging note that said things were going well and to keep up the pressure. It seemed right that I'd come to Cape Town, and I was doing all that I could. I was beginning to entertain less dire scenarios at this point, but I was still very cautious.

The next day, I received a faxed copy of the letter of intent to provide funding, also called a comfort letter, from the chairman of the SBA lender. It was just in time, because my meeting with the SAFJC was scheduled for the next Tuesday, November 5. On November 2, Edgar called and said he had talked to the chairman of the SAFJC. He said the chairman had been unaware of the situation but understood the "political gravity of the situation," as he expressed it. He said the chairman had become uncomfortable when he'd learned about my meetings with the government ministers and had expressed concern about the situation escalating, especially in view of the SAFJC's recent court battle with their union. He had asked Edgar whether I would be "reasonable."

It sounded to me that I was in a good position because the company could not afford to alienate me given the high-profile issues they were dealing with. Later that day, I met with three black businessmen who had been referred by the government minister's office. They too expressed a willingness to attend the Tuesday meeting with me. Among other things, they warned me that I should not refer to myself as a black woman. I didn't understand this. I couldn't pretend to be someone I wasn't. They told me that the SAFJC only employed "colored" people in the factories, so it was very difficult for some Afrikaners to openly report that they were doing business with a black woman, even one from the United States. (Colored people were those of mixed racial heritage and were on the second rung of the apartheid system, one step above a black person who was of black African descent.)

The knot in my stomach now turned into a fiery pain. I had never gotten the impression from Pieter that I couldn't call myself a black woman. I had always been treated well. My mind was spinning. *They think I'm a bitch, I can't call myself black—so what do I do now? Clearly, there are a lot of different opinions about what is going on. Perhaps I underestimated the sociopolitical aspect of all this. I have to see this through; the high government official is involved, the SAFJC board all know that this is going on. They have to at least be courteous to me; don't they? Of course they do.*

Reality Check: Your mind will spin with as many thoughts as you allow; the only important thing is your response. What were my real concerns? Did I have any options at this point?

The only thing I could do was to go into the meeting well prepared. I had all my papers with me. I had documentation about when the orders had been placed and the bills of lading supporting my claim that they had breached the contract by not getting product to me on time as per the distribution agreement.

I called Edgar again. He said it appeared that the SAFJC would be very amenable to resolving the situation. However, he advised that I should not have the government minister's director or the black businessmen attend the meeting with me. Nor should I have Jacoline send the letter from the high government official. "Why?" I'd spent all this time assembling allies, and now it looked like a total waste of time.

Edgar explained that the SAFJC was a private company and would not appreciate any outside involvement. He also advised that my conversation with them should not focus on the outstanding money, but rather on the SAFJC's commitment to Bethington Enterprises and their failure to provide product in a timely manner.

As I was taking all this in, Edgar briskly informed me that he would not be able to attend the meeting after all. Also, the chairman of the SAFJC would not be attending the meeting because of the delicate relationship between him and Willem, the managing director. Before I could ask any more questions, Edgar said goodbye, promising to call me on Tuesday to see how the meeting had gone.

Things had clearly changed. I was disappointed. Despite the support I'd carefully built over the past week, it looked like I was on my own, and I didn't understand why.

THE MEETING

November 5 was the big day. In the meeting, the SAFJC was represented by four people: Pieter, the director of international markets; Willem, the managing director; Thomas, a black SAFJC board member; and Abraham, the SAFJC's attorney. Based on Edgar's advice, I was only represented by my US attorney, who was remotely wired in, and my newly appointed South African attorney, whom I hardly knew.

The meeting began rather contentiously but got better as we went along. The bottom line was that the SAFJC was willing to enter into a new agreement with Bethington Enterprises based on the new payment provision of a letter of credit (versus the current 90-day open account terms) and their commitment to get product to me within eight weeks, as stipulated in the previous agreement.

I informed them of my commitment from the Philadelphia bank for a letter of credit financing and presented the comfort letter from the bank president. They were very happy to see that I had the capacity to pay the outstanding debt. I stressed that the financing was predicated on a firm contractual relationship with the SAFJC and a letter from them indicating their full support of me as their distributor in the United States. Although the SAFJC did acknowledge their production problems, they never seemed to take responsibility for its impact on my business. From my point of view, based on my claims for repacking costs and short-dated product, I didn't owe them any money. However, from their point of view, I did.

> Reality Check: Should your supplier take responsibility for the impact their production issues have on their distributors? Was it objective for me to think so?

Trying to look to the future, as Edgar had advised, I raised the possibility of the SAFJC buying equity in Bethington Enterprises in an attempt to develop a partnership relationship. Thomas and Willem seemed interested in this, which I took as encouraging. They indicated that the SAFJC was considering central distribution in the United States. I presented Willem with a copy of the proposal I had submitted to Pieter in June 1996 for central distribution. He was impressed and, much to my surprise, indicated that Pieter had never presented him with the proposal.

The upshot of the meeting was that they agreed to provide me with a letter indicating the SAFJC commitment to Bethington Enterprises. We further agreed that I would not leave South Africa until the situation was resolved, i.e., the agreement was signed, the letter was presented, and the financing was in place.

When the meeting ended, I felt hopeful. Although they had not yet agreed to my claim for short-dated product, they had agreed to continue doing business with me. As I was leaving the building, Thomas told me that he had a meeting at Stellenbosch. I asked him if he knew Edgar. "Of course," he said, "Edgar has been doing consulting work with us for years."

I then told him what he already knew, namely that I'd had lunch with Edgar on the previous Wednesday. Thomas looked at me, laughed, and said, "Your contacts may have conflicts of interests."

My God, I thought, *what am I doing mixed up in all of this?* The knot in my stomach flared. My hopefulness quickly turned to dread.

We all agreed to get back together two days later to resolve the issue of the claim for short-dated product and to flesh out the broad strokes of a new distribution agreement. On my way out, Willem pulled me aside and said, "Elizabeth, we just never thought you would do this well. None of the other suppliers did anything significant with this juice."

Frankly, I did not know how to respond. I said, "Thank you, I really believe that it is a great product and it will do well in the United States." But deep down, I was wondering. Was it a compliment? Or was I just a thorn in their side that they couldn't get rid of? Why sign a five-year distribution agreement with me, agree to formally launch the product in the United States with me, and not think I would do this well? Clearly, I challenged whatever mental models they held about the US distribution of their product—and about me.

On Thursday morning before my second meeting with SAFJC, I woke up to a fax from my assistant back home saying that she had received a call from one of the other US distributors wondering if Bethington Enterprises was still in business. Apparently, Pieter had sent a memo to the United States and Canadian distributors that had excluded Bethington Enterprises. I didn't know what to make of this. How could they exclude me if they were negotiating in good faith? Or was it a meaningless omission?

I arrived at SAFJC feeling a bit gut-punched but determined to present myself in a professional and friendly manner. This time, Willem, the managing director, and their attorney were the only ones representing the SAFJC. My South African attorney and my US attorney, who was on the phone, again represented me. The demeanor of the SAFJC representatives appeared to be friendlier, but they agreed to provide only 20 percent of my claim for the short-dated product. I negotiated for them to meet me halfway. However, my main concern was getting product shipped immediately to the United States to avoid running out of inventory for my customers. But they stated they would release the product only when the bill was paid and the letter of credit was set up for the new order.

Equally friendly in my demeanor, I expressed my concern that these negotiations were one-sided; they were about the SAFJC getting paid and eliminating all of their risks via the letter of credit. It seemed that there were no provisions for eliminating my risk of running out of inventory to meet customer orders or the cost of carrying large amounts of inventory to offset their production inefficiencies.

In reply, they said they were working on the production issue. They also said they all recognized my company's results, but in their view Pieter had risked his job by extending me 90-day open-account terms versus a letter of credit, and that I had taken advantage of him.

I did not understand that line of reasoning. I also told them about the fax I received from home that morning and asked about the memo they had sent to the other distributors that excluded Bethington Enterprises. The SAFJC attorney appeared appalled at this news, and said that they would correct this right away. My attorney expressed his concern over what he called "egregious behavior."

The meeting adjourned with Bethington Enterprises committed to sending a revised distribution agreement with my preferred terms to the SAFJC's attorney by the end of the next day. Based on my input, the SAFJC agreed to write a letter of support of Bethington Enterprises as their distributor that I could send to United Bank to secure the financing.

> Reality Check: At this point, do I understand my suppliers' point of view or frame of reference? What do they want? What is their goal? Am I looking at this from only my point of view?

By this time, I needed to have a small amount of product, only one container of specific flavors, shipped out of South Africa by the next day. According to my staff, we were dangerously close to not being able to fill the order of our largest distributor. I was concerned about how long it would take for the SAFJC and me to come to terms on the agreement, get the financing in place, and ship the product. That Thursday, I left the meeting worried, but still hoping things could be resolved.

WAITING

Then, all of a sudden, things seemed to stall, and I didn't understand why. The SAFJC postponed the Friday meeting where we'd agreed to discuss the terms and where they were to give me a letter of support. For ten days, I waited in Cape Town for the SAFJC to get back to me. The Diplomat was frustrated, too, and did not know what more he could do. He suggested that I fly to Johannesburg to personally meet with Jacoline, the legal advisor (general counsel) of the high government official. Not knowing what else to do, I flew to Johannesburg on November 18. The goal was to fully brief her on everything that had transpired so she could determine if there was any further legal recourse; if so, would it be possible for The Diplomat and other members of the new South African government to testify on my behalf? But as it turned out, since the contract was based in South African law and the supplier was a South African company, The Diplomat and the other ministers, as employees of South Africa, could not testify against their own country.

I was feeling very sad. I'd been stuck in South Africa for almost a month waiting for a new distribution agreement, and by now it was pretty clear that the SAFJC did not want to do business with Elizabeth Thornton, a.k.a. the Fruit Juice Lady—because she was and was not black and had performed better than expected even though she could and could not be a bitch. And something—I didn't know what—was clearly going on with the Afrikaner company in Canada.

Thanksgiving was the following week. My visa was expiring, and I needed to get the heck out of the country, get home, and at least have time to liquidate my inventory. My only goal now was to get a piece of paper from the SAFJC that said I was a distributor so I could at least do that. I had employees and other obligations that I needed to honor. The knot in my stomach had gone away. I was just numb.

Finally, on November 29, I met with the SAFJC. They handed me an agreement with a clause that said that I would remain a distributor until such time as they adopt a new supply method or distribution method, which might entail appointing a central Canadian-based supplier or distributing agent for the overall US market.

When I read this part of the agreement, I was angry. Something had gone so wrong, and I didn't understand what had happened. I took the papers and said I'd have my attorney review them. A few days later, when I called The Diplomat and explained what had transpired, he was so angry he called it subterfuge and a whitewash. "Don't sign the agreement," he said.

I was disoriented at this point. On December 3, I signed the agreement so I could get back to the United States and hang in there long enough to pay my employees and some of my debt. I wanted to go home. Before leaving I called Thomas, the black SAFJC board member, to thank him for his support. He told me why the negotiations had stalled mysteriously for six weeks.

On November 18, while I was meeting with Jacoline in Johannesburg, Willem, the managing director of the SAFJC, had met with all the other agents, including the Afrikaner company from Canada. Apparently, the memo that was sent to the distributors that excluded Bethington Enterprises had requested the distributors to fly to Cape Town for a meeting on November 18, at which the SAFJC informed them that the Afrikaner company from Canada was taking over all of North America as their central distributor. I thanked Thomas for being so candid, but I felt punched in the stomach. It was truly over.

SHUTTING DOWN A FAILED BUSINESS

On December 5, I finally flew back home. I started liquidating my inventory. I had to take care of my employees. The good news was that while I was in South Africa, I had written a detailed chronology of every meeting and every conversation and had faxed updates to The Diplomat every other day.

I went on another road show, this time without the juice, and told everyone who ever supported me in the business that I was out of business. I met with each distributor, broker, and creditor, and explained what had happened. I was surprised and so very grateful that all the people to whom I owed money forgave the debt, including the advertising agency. People said they had seen me walk through a wall to try to do this, they saw how successful it had become in a very short period of time, and that these were circumstances I could not control. So that was a bit of a silver lining.

I met with Ted, my dearest friend and the lead investor, and presented him with the chronology of events. While angry and disappointed, he'd come to believe that the deal was rigged from the start.

He wanted me to move on, so he said he would handle all the communications to the investor group. This was the hardest conversation for me because Ted had put his reputation and his relationships on the line for me. I told him then that I didn't know when or how, but I was going to find a way to pay him and all the other investors back—not a return *on* their investment, but a return *of* their investment.

After having all of these difficult and painful conversations, I was home alone and it finally sunk in. I had risked everything and lost everything trying to save South Africa. I lost my condo in New York, my savings, and even my stock portfolio. I was so broke; I remember searching for change deep behind the sofa cushion for enough money to drive to Philadelphia so that I could meet my other brother. He gave me $300, and I was at least able to put gas in my car and buy groceries. For days and weeks, I went over everything in my mind to understand what the heck just happened. Sometime later, someone from Ted Koppel's office called and wanted to speak to me about a story they were thinking of doing about my experience in South Africa. I met with them, but my ego would not allow it. I did not want to be that new person, to take on a new identity: *the woman who lost everything in South Africa.* I was still angry. I wanted answers. My mind wouldn't rest.

I finally gave up and accepted the fact that it was truly over. I was deeply depressed and clearly paralyzed. I was no longer who I thought I was. Now that I wasn't the Fruit Juice Lady or CEO of a marketing consulting company, who was I? I remember going outside and looking around and thinking, *My world has just come to an end, yet the world is still going on. I don't understand that.* If rock bottom is as low as one can go, then I had found a new place—somewhere well below the rock.

MOVIE MARATHONS AND COMFORT FOOD

Fortunately, I got up from that. It took me awhile. After many months of watching movie marathons to avoid thinking, and eating lots of popcorn and vanilla chip ice cream, I finally got off the couch and began putting my life back together. I got a job and was able to function in the world again. But I kept asking myself a lot of questions. How could a successful person who had not only never failed, but achieved some level of success in the corporate world at a relatively young age, crash and burn so badly? Why didn't I see this coming before it was too late? What could

I have done differently? I remembered the old saying, "What doesn't kill you will make you stronger," and I asked myself, how can I make sure I am stronger from this? How do I know I won't fail again? After months of self-reflection, I had to admit to myself that I had often experienced hiccups along the way, although not to this extreme. By hiccups, I mean times when things were going along just fine, and then all of a sudden they weren't. But now I needed answers. If I didn't understand what I had done or why, then it was possible I could do it all again and maybe self-destruct—even worse.

Over the next several years I continued searching for answers. It wasn't just about how I lost a million dollars. My questions were more fundamental: Who was I, if not the job I had or the role I played? I started with psychology, studying when and how one's self-image is developed. Then I moved to sociology and learned how social norms and mores are established, reinforced, and rewarded over time. I studied Western philosophers such as Kant, Descartes, Locke, Plato, and Aristotle, seeking to understand the philosophical underpinnings of perception and reality. I then spent years studying Eastern philosophy, taking a deep dive into the Bhagavad Gita and the Upanishads, seeking to understand the nature of the Self and the connection between me, others, and the world. Next, I turned to the study of neuroscience to understand how the mind and brain worked. Finally, I looked to quantum physics to get a sense of the latest science regarding cognition, matter, and reality. When I began to reflect on and synthesize all these ideas, I realized that the core reason I had hiccups along the way, and ultimately crashed and burned, was because of my *inherent subjectivity*. The problem did not stem so much from the business decisions I did or did not make, but in how I framed my world—the underlying assumptions that drove my perceptions and responses to the people, circumstances, and events in my life. What I learned was that being happy, effective, and successful requires wrestling with my inherent subjectivity and practicing objectivity, which can be simply defined as "seeing things as they are."

With this new understanding, it was clear to me that if I wanted to respond differently, I had to change my mind about what I fundamentally believed about myself, others, and the world. I began to reevaluate all my assumptions and found that the way I was framing my world was not serving me very well. Things that I learned and accepted as true when I was younger were no longer true for me, yet these assumptions were still guiding my behavior. I found that many of my ideas and beliefs were based in insecurity, fear, and self-doubt and that these beliefs were clouding my perception and interpretation of everything I experienced. The fear-based lens through which I perceived the world did not just contribute to my failed business; it was also negatively affecting my interactions with the people in my life.

I finally understood that my experience of the world was, in fact, in my mind. As determined as I was to save South Africa and to be the Fruit Juice Lady, I was even more determined now to change the lens through which I perceived and responded to my world. I knew that my happiness and my success depended on my ability to be objective, to see and accept things as they are. After a lot of honest and painful self-reflection, I was able to rethink many of my fear- and insecurity-based beliefs. Over time, I was able to rebuild my self-concept so that it was less dependent on other's approval. I began to redefine not only who I was, but also *what* I was relative to everything and everyone else. I also began to reassess how I valued myself so that my self-worth was less tied to the job I had, the title I held, or the role I played. I began to value and appreciate myself for who I was, not what I did, and along the way, my relationships got better. For the first time in a very long time, I felt happy and fearless.

BACK IN THE SADDLE AGAIN

Squarely back on my feet and armed with a powerful experience of entrepreneurship, especially what not to do, I began seeking new opportunities to make a difference. In the fall of 2006, Babson College, ranked number

1 in the nation for entrepreneurship education for the last 21 consecutive years by *U.S. News and World Report*, hired me to teach entrepreneurship in their graduate, undergraduate, and executive education programs. Babson was where I first publicly shared the story of how I lost the million dollars. What I had learned was so much more than what is taught in a traditional business school case study about a failed business.

In 2008, with the encouragement and support of many of my colleagues at Babson, I compiled everything that I had studied and learned and developed an entrepreneurship elective entitled "The Principle of Objectivity." The course is now one of the most popular electives at the F. W. Olin Graduate School of Business at Babson. In addition, I now conduct corporate training programs through Babson's Executive Education, teaching senior management teams how objectivity is a core competency for effective leadership. This book has grown out of that curriculum.

My goal now is to share with you what I have learned about the power of seeing things as they are. As we begin, please remember to have an open mind and try to validate everything you are reading with your own direct experience. With your commitment to self-reflection, I promise this book can inspire you to change your life in amazing ways...without the need to experience a disorienting event like losing a million dollars.

Part II

YOU CAN'T BE MAD AT YOUR MIND

Chapter 2

UNDERSTANDING SUBJECTIVITY

Clearly, lack of objectivity can have enormous consequences. Looking back on it now, I can easily see that if I had been more objective, I would not have lost so much, fewer people would have been impacted, and I may have rebounded more quickly. We will examine the key lessons learned and the missed opportunities to respond more objectively as we go along. In the meantime, can you think of situations where in hindsight you wish you had responded more objectively? What did it cost you?

Leadership effectiveness is measured by our ability to achieve results. We analyze the situation, make a decision, take action, and hope for the desired result. Our results are determined by the actions we take. Our actions are determined by the decisions we make. Our decisions are based on what we think or believe about the situation. The challenge for leaders is that it is quite natural for us to perceive and respond to everything we experience through the lens of our mental models. These mental models are our deep-rooted ideas, assumptions, and biases about the way the world works and how things ought to be. When we encounter a person, situation or event, we instantly project our mental models, which are often based on our backgrounds, past experiences, and fears. The end result is that we often perceive, judge, and respond to people, circumstances, and events incorrectly, and we fail to achieve our intended result. Our ability to evaluate situations, make decisions, and take effective action is directly related to our ability to be *objective*—to perceive and respond to things as they really are.

The truth is, our inherent subjectivity impacts our effectiveness each and every day, in all aspects of our lives. I'm currently conducting a quantitative and qualitative study of objectivity in which I survey and interview participants of my objectivity classes, workshops, or seminars. Interestingly, we have learned that overreactions to people, circumstances, or events are quite common, regardless of the respondent's gender. (Yes, it appears that men do this as often as women!) In fact, a summary of the data suggests that 89.1 percent of respondents said they overreacted once per month or more, 21.9 percent admitted they overreacted 2 or 3 times per month, 23.4 percent admitted to overreacting once per week, 14.1 percent said they overreacted 2 or 3 times per week, and 6.3 percent said they overreacted every day. Sometimes we can recover from these overreactions, but sometimes we cannot; the damage is already done.

How often do you overreact? The first step toward increasing your objectivity is to honestly reflect on how often and in what situations you are less than objective. To stimulate your thinking, here is an extreme example of how an overreaction can spiral out of control at work. Put yourself in Jim's shoes.

Jim has been in his new job for six months. He has always been conscientious and hardworking. He is considered to be on the fast track. Every morning around 7:45 a.m., Scott, Jim's boss, passes by Jim's desk with a warm and boisterous "Good morning, Jim." But one day, Scott walks by Jim's desk and just nods.

Jim's mind starts spinning with the following thoughts:

I heard there may be lay-offs. Scott has probably been told by his boss that he has to reduce headcount. I've only been with the company for six months. I'm the employee in the department with the least tenure, so Scott has no choice but to fire me. He didn't say hello because he feels bad about it. I'm about to lose my job, which means not only no new toys for my son and no new coat for my wife, but now I'll lose my family because they'll leave me if I can no longer support them.

As a result of these increasingly negative thoughts, Jim becomes so anxious that he runs into Scott's office and bursts out: "Are there going to be layoffs soon? Am I on the list?" Scott laughs, shakes his head. "What are you talking about? Just relax. No one's said anything about layoffs."

Jim reacted to his boss's subdued greeting from a position of subjectivity. He jumped to conclusions and overreacted. Had he evaluated the situation more clearly, he would have begun by looking at the facts: every morning around 7 a.m. for many months, Scott passed Jim's desk with a warm and boisterous greeting. Today Scott passed Jim's desk without saying hello. Period. End of story.

Instead, Jim evaluated this situation through the lens of his fears and insecurities, which caused him to perceive, interpret, and respond incorrectly. Were his fears irrational? No, not really. Although the economy has improved, many people are still concerned about losing their jobs. Acting on his fears by running down the hall and cornering his boss is the problem. He did not even think about other ways to evaluate and respond to the situation. As Jim later learned, his boss's 20-year-old daughter had just been injured in a car accident. Scott was too preoccupied to give Jim his usual boisterous greeting. Unfortunately, after this incident, Scott saw Jim as impetuous, unstable, and reactionary. Jim's reputation suffered.

The research also suggests that we often take things personally and respond defensively, which can blind us to the truth of the situation. When we asked workshop participants how often they took things personally, 92.2 percent of respondents said at least once a month or more, 21.9 percent said 2 or 3 times per month, 12.5 percent said once per week, 23.4 percent said 2 or 3 times per week, and 12.5 percent said daily. How often are you taking things personally? Do you do so more at work or more at home? Again, let's look at another extreme case of subjectivity and how taking things personally can influence personal relationships.

Patricia and Sam have been dating for four months. Things are wonderful; they have so much in common. A match made in heaven. Every morning around eight, on his way to work, Sam calls Patricia to wish her a good day and to tell her that he loves her. "Have a good day sweetheart, I love you" is the morning sign-off. One morning Sam doesn't call Patricia on the way to work. It is 9 a.m., and Patricia is naturally quite concerned that she has not heard from Sam. She is worried that something awful has happened to him—a car accident or something even worse. Finally, around 9:30, Sam calls Patricia and apologizes for not calling her earlier. He seems a little distant. He says that he will call her later. Patricia is quite upset. She is thinking to herself:

Sam did not say "I love you," so obviously he is seeing someone else. While I'm sitting here wondering whether he is hurt on the side of the road somewhere, he got to work late because he was out last night with someone new. I do think he cared for me, but he probably fell in love unexpectedly with this person and is now afraid of hurting my feelings. He knows how much I care for him, so he won't want to tell me at work because he knows I'll be too upset. I think I'll call him back, let him off the hook, and tell him I think we should start seeing other people.

She called Sam and very abruptly broke up with him.

In this case the only thing that happened was that Sam did not call at eight, and when he finally did call, he didn't say I love you. That's it. Patricia projected her past experience onto the current situation, and her mind concocted a painful reason for his not calling. She was devastated in her prior relationship by a man who broke up with her, so she perceived everything through the lens of her past experience. It turns out Sam got a flat tire on the way to work. Knowing the tires were bald, he was embarrassed to tell Patricia. Her lack of objectivity cost her a potentially good relationship.

Can you relate to either of these situations? Have you ever done anything like this?

Unfortunately, our inherent subjectivity does not just impact us as individuals at work or at home; it can impact large groups of people. Though we have come to expect some degree of subjectivity from our politicians, the events leading up to and throughout the government shutdown was a perfect example of subjectivity run amok. When the crisis started, a small group of Republicans was unable to accept the reality that the Affordable Care Act, which passed both the House and the Senate, was affirmed with the 2012 election and upheld by the Supreme Court, and would go into effect October 1, 2013. We've all been there. It's that moment when you want so badly for something not to have happened that your brain jumps through every mental hoop in the book to conceive and force a different reality. It never works. This small group of Republicans decided to shut down the government to try to force Democrats to amend the Affordable Care Act. Of course, this reckless act took on a momentum of its own, and many people's lives were negatively affected—and the outcome was unchanged.

The bottom line is that we often do not see things as they are. Our vision of reality is often distorted by our past experience, our mental models, and our expectations. How, then, can we be effective leaders, make sound judgments, and execute effectively?

OBJECTIVITY: IS IT POSSIBLE TO BE MORE OBJECTIVE?

The real question is: Is true objectivity possible? Philosophers have been debating the epistemological underpinnings of objectivity and subjectivity for centuries. Epistemology is the branch of philosophy that studies the nature of knowledge and truth. Epistemologists explore questions such as: What is knowledge? What does it mean for someone to know something? Is there an ultimate ground of knowledge, a world of absolutes? Do we know something from reason, or from direct observation, or from a little of both? What is the relationship between the observer and the observed, the knower and the known?

Great thinkers such as Locke, Kant, Descartes, Aristotle, and Plato debated whether there is such a thing as an objective reality. They distinguished between things that exist subjectively (dependent upon the mind) and objectively (independent of the mind). Kant, for example, stated that the world we experience is shaped by our minds. He states that we can know truth only in relation to our mind, or as it appears in the objects of the world. Some have concluded that you can only know if something is objectively real if a group of rationally minded people can verify it. Others, like John Wheeler, an American theoretical physicist, went so far as to say that the world is a projection of the mind, that there is no objective reality, there is no "out there" out there, and it is all mind-dependent. In one of his famous quotes, Wheeler said, "The universe does not exist 'out there,' independent of us. We are inescapably involved in bringing about that which appears to be happening. We are not only observers. We are participators."[1]

Even today, there is a spirited debate among neuroscientists, psychologists, and neurologists about whether there is such a thing as an autonomous rational mind. Daniel Goleman's *Emotional Intelligence*, Malcolm Gladwell's *Blink*, and Robert Burton's *On Being Certain* are all thought-provoking books on the nature of the mind, including the elusive and often unknowable subconscious. Burton talks about the sense of knowing and how we know what we know, the reality of rational thought, and the value and limitations of self-reflection. Recent books, such as *Incognito* by David Eagleman, a national best seller, *The Hidden Brain* by Shankar Vedantam, and *The Tell-Tale Brain* by V. S. Ramachandran all espouse a new understanding of the brain from a neuroscientific perspective that challenges the way we have been taught to think about what we perceive and how we respond to it.

From everything I have studied about the philosophy, psychology, and science behind objectivity; from what I have learned through my research, teaching, and executive coaching; and from my own experience, I have concluded that it is indeed possible to increase one's objectivity. I believe, from an empirical perspective, that there *is* an objective reality. I call it "It Is Therefore I See"—in other words, everything that is part of our world, for which we can say that It Is, whether we see, hear, touch, taste, smell it or not.

For example, the other day I was driving to a meeting. I got off the highway and started following an unfamiliar route in the city. I was thinking about what I wanted to say at the meeting, who would be there—everything but the driving. All of a sudden I heard a loud thud and was bounced uncomfortably on my seat. My car had hit a pothole. Nothing I could do or say or feel would change the objective reality of that pothole. Whether I see it or not, It Is.

Even though empirically I believe there is an objective reality, I do not believe we, as humans, can be 100 percent objective. As Burton wrote in his book *On Being Certain*: "complete objectivity is not an option."[2] We are all subjective about the way we *respond* to "what is": the people we encounter, the circumstances in our lives, and ourselves. What we *can* do is reduce our subjectivity, what I call "I See, Therefore It Is"—in other words, our projections, the things we invent about a situation, person, or event. And we make up so much! In the case of Jim, he projected his fears onto the fact that his boss did not respond in his usual way. In my case with the South African Fruit Juice Company, I projected my mental models about business onto the supplier and responded to the unfolding problems through that lens.

It's even the simplest things, like walking down the street. Have you ever passed someone on the street and wondered why they looked at you funny? In this case, we see what we decide is a funny look and exclaim that It Is. In most cases, the person was just pensive, thinking about something other than you, and just happened to be looking in your direction. How about this? Have you ever perceived a negative tone in an e-mail at work, assumed the sender was attacking you, and then you attacked back and sent an e-mail with a negative tone? These are the things we make up. We make it real, part of our reality, our experience, and we respond as if IT IS.

The good news is that we can challenge our underlying assumptions and the way we frame our world in order to reduce our subjectivity and respond more objectively to what actually *is*. We can learn to be clear about and respond to objective reality. When we can see things as they are, without projecting our mental models and fears, we are being objective. When we can ask ourselves about other possible ways of looking at a situation, we are being objective. When we can understand and consider another person's point of view, we are being objective. When we can identify and evaluate assumptions and conclusions other than our own, we are being objective. When we can put our past experience behind us, use it only as a data point but evaluate situations in the present, we are being objective. Therefore our working definition of objectivity is *seeing and accepting things as they are without projecting our fears, mental models, and past experiences, and responding thoughtfully and deliberately to the people, circumstances, and events in our lives.*

The purpose of this book is to help you increase your objectivity. The first exercise is to establish your personal baseline by acknowledging how objective you currently are, and in what circumstances you tend to be more subjective. Once you have established your baseline, the next step is to understand how you relate to the world.

ACTION PLAN: EXERCISE 1

ASSESSING YOUR CURRENT LEVEL OF OBJECTIVITY AND PINPOINTING YOUR HOT SPOTS (WHEN YOU ARE MORE SUBJECTIVE).

To start the process of increasing objectivity, begin by assessing how often you might respond less than objectively:

- How many times a day, week, or month do you overreact to situations?
- How many times a day, week, or month do you take things personally?

Once you have a sense of how often you are making cognitive errors, the next step is to pinpoint your hot spots by identifying what types of situations or interactions you are least objective about. Describe a professional situation where you were less than objective. Jot down your answers to the following questions:

- What is the objective reality of what happened?
- What was the cognitive error? What did you think was happening?
- What was your response?
- Looking back, what could have been a more appropriate response?
- What did it cost you?

Please repeat this exercise for a personal situation.

Chapter 3

THE SUBJECT–OBJECT RELATIONSHIP

How We Relate to the World

It is important to understand the subject-object relationship—that is, how we relate to the world—before we can understand why it is indeed possible to increase our objectivity.

It works like this: you are the Subject ("I"), and everything else is the object ("other" or "not I"). For example, you are the Subject and this book is an object to you. As the Subject, you perceive the world through your five senses: sight, hearing, taste, smell, and touch. Our senses connect us to the world. Our world is alive with stimuli—all the people, objects, and events that surround us. "Sensation and perception are the processes that allow us to detect and understand these various stimuli. Sensation is the process of converting a stimulus from the external environment, such as temperature, into a signal transported along the appropriate neural pathway. Physical energy, in the form of light, sound, and heat, is detected by specialized receptor cells in the sense organs—eyes, ears, skin, nose, and tongue, and relayed through the sensory nerves to the spinal cord and brain.

Perception is the process of organizing and interpreting sensory information so that it makes sense. The mind collects, deciphers, and integrates all the information we receive through our senses and constructs our conscious perception."[1] Without the mind, perception does not actually happen. That is why you can look directly in someone's eyes and appear to be listening, yet you really have no idea what the person said. Your mind was elsewhere. The mind must be behind the eyes, otherwise you will not see. The mind must be behind the ears because the ears by themselves do not hear. Thus sensation and perception, the senses and the mind, work hand in hand. "For example, receptor cells in our eyes record—that is, sense—a sleek silver object in the sky, but they do not 'see' a jet plane. Recognizing that silver object as a plane is perception."[2]

The question is, given our sensation-perception interaction with the world, are we ever totally objective? From an empirical perspective, yes, we are objective every day. For example, you are walking along a path and you come across a bed of roses. You see the roses; there is the sensation of sight, sight takes place. You have no choice in the matter. If the flower is there and your eyes are open and working properly, and your mind is behind your eyes, conscious of what the eyes see, then you will perceive the roses. What choice do you have to smell an odor that you would rather not smell? Again, none. We are objective when we receive data through our senses of "what is."

However, after our initial sensory experience of "what is," things tend to get a little murky. Many of us have taken for granted that we perceive the world as it actually is, but in fact, we do not. We now know that our perception can be influenced by many factors. When we sense the object, our immediate perception, interpretation, and response to the object or situation is subjective. Our perception is mind-dependent, conditioned by our mental models, our expectations, our fears, our past experiences, et cetera. I call these *drivers of subjectivity*. Often we are unaware of these drivers; they lie beneath our conscious awareness. This is the reason we sometimes don't understand why we respond the way we do, especially in loaded situations. This is also why two people can experience the same object through their senses, yet their perception of it and response to it are often very different. Their perception and response are based on their individual drivers of subjectivity.

So what is the point of all this? You are the Subject and everything else is an object of your knowledge, perception, or awareness, and therefore *not* you. What it means is that as the Subject, you are ultimately responsible for how you respond to everything you experience. Although some people may try, no one can dictate your response to any person, situation, or event, or anything else that you experience. It's up to you, every time, because it is your mind that determines your interpretation or perception of it, which drives your response to it.

As such, the key to increasing your objectivity is to own your cognitive appraisal process by being consciously aware of it as much as possible and responding purposefully rather than automatically to the people and circumstances of your life. As the Subject, you have the power to do that, and believe me, leveraging that power will distinguish you at work and at home. As the Subject, you have the power to see things as they are, to reduce cognitive errors, make better decisions, and create new possibilities for your life.

In the next section, we will see how it is natural for us to be subjective, but it is within the capacity of the brain to increase our objectivity. We will start with a brief overview of the brain in simple layman's terms.

AN APPRECIATION FOR THE MIND AND OUR SUBJECTIVITY

Our brains are pattern-making organs, made up of 100 billion nerve cells called neurons. "These neurons have spidery branches that reach out and connect to other neurons to form neural networks. A typical neuron has about 10,000 connections, or associations, with neighboring neurons, making a total of some 100 trillion connections."[3] To put this in context, NASA's latest estimates for the number of stars in the Milky Way Galaxy is somewhere between 200 and 400 billion.

From the time we are children, our minds are rapidly forming associations, drawing conclusions about everything we experience through sensory input, and creating connections in our neural networks. Scientists believe the synapses, the places where neurons connect, play an instrumental role in memory. As these neural connections strengthen and fire together, memory is reinforced. Ideas, thoughts, and feelings are all constructed and interconnected in the neural net, and all have a potential relationship with one another. Our expectations and experiences of happiness, love, and success, for example, become hardwired in the neural net as a result of our histories, experiences, and emotional responses to those experiences.

Our brains are continually gathering information and steering behavior based on these associations and connections, steadily building a neural structure. This structure is constantly changing as we experience and adapt to the world around us. Our brains do all of this automatically, constantly pruning connections while making new ones, without our conscious awareness.

Scientists have delineated the activities of the brain into two types: conscious and unconscious, or activities of which we are aware and ones beneath our conscious awareness. In *The Hidden Brain*, Shankar Vedantam suggests that we have both a hidden brain and a conscious brain because we regularly encounter two kinds of experiences, those that are new and those that are familiar. The hidden brain (the unconscious activities of the brain) deals with the familiar, and the conscious brain (the conscious activities of the brain) deals with the new and the novel. The conscious brain is rational, careful, and analytical.[4] It is slow and deliberate. The conscious brain engages our working memory, "the brain's holding area, where perceptions and ideas are compared to other information," when we encounter something new. For example, when you see an advertisement for the latest smartphone and rationally compare its benefits to your existing phone, it is your working memory, part of your conscious mind that takes in the new information and matches it against the old.[5] This category of memory activates the prefrontal cortex, an energy-intensive part of the brain. Daniel G. Amen, a psychiatrist and brain-imaging specialist, describes the prefrontal cortex in his book *Change Your Brain, Change Your Life* as follows: "[It is] the most evolved part of the brain. Overall, the prefrontal cortex is the part of the brain that watches, supervises, guides, directs and focuses our behavior. It supervises 'executive functions,' governing abilities such as time management, judgment, impulse control, planning, organization, and critical thinking. Our ability as a species to think, plan ahead, use time wisely, and communicate with others is heavily influenced by this part of the brain. The prefrontal cortex is responsible for behaviors that are necessary for us to be goal-directed, socially responsible and effective."[6]

The process when we encounter something new involves the conscious brain. But once a problem is understood and the rule to solve it is discovered, it makes no sense to think through the problem afresh every time you encounter it. You apply the rules you learned and move on. This is where the hidden brain comes in. Shankar Vedantam describes it as "a master of heuristic, the mental shortcuts we use to carry out the boring stuff."[7]

The hidden brain contains the basal ganglia, a set of large structures near the center of the brain. One structure called the caudate is responsible for accuracy and speed of voluntary movements. It works with the other structure called the putamen to coordinate automatic actions. "The integration of feelings, thoughts, and movement occurs in the basal ganglia. This is why you jump when you're excited, tremble when you're nervous, freeze when you are scared, or get tongue-tied when the boss is chewing you out."[8] The hidden brain is invoked by routine, familiar activity like putting an often-purchased product into a supermarket cart. It's your basal ganglia that enables you, after 20 years, to still ride a bike. This is because of the principle in neuroscience called Hebb's law: Basically, "nerve cells that are wired together, fire together."[9] This means that every time we practice something, groups of nerve cells are repeatedly activated together, creating long-term relationships among them that form a neural circuit.

The basal ganglia requires much less energy to function than working memory does, because it seamlessly links simple behaviors from brain modules that have already been shaped by the repetitive experience. In contrast, working memory fatigues easily and can only handle a limited amount of information at one time.

This is how it works when you learn something new. When you first ride a bicycle, you pay conscious attention to your balance, your speed, and how hard you are peddling so that you don't fall off. But once you master how the rules of gravity, balance, and momentum interact, your conscious brain relegates bike riding to the hidden brain, specifically to the basal ganglia. You no longer have to think about what you are doing, and it becomes automatic. This frees up processing power for your working memory and the prefrontal cortex.

So, just as riding a bike or driving a car have become routine, so too have many of our responses to the things we encounter each day. How we respond to e-mails, how we behave in team meetings, how we approach new projects—it all becomes automatic over time. Here's how it works when you encounter these familiar situations: "Your brain conserves the energy of working memory by shifting into a kind of automatic pilot. You then rely on long established neural connections in the basal ganglia that have, in effect, become hardwired for this situation and your response to it. This makes it easy for you to do the same thing you have always done, and frees you to do two things at once…multitask."[10] How much of what you do each day have you shifted to automatic pilot? How often are you multitasking?

To increase our objectivity, we must bring more of our automatic reactions—those that are hardwired and relegated to the basal ganglia—up to conscious scrutiny and analysis by the prefrontal cortex *before* we respond.

THE MIND AND MENTAL MODELS

Embedded in our neural net are mental models. Mental models are deep-rooted ideas and beliefs that we have about ourselves, the way the world works, and how things ought to be. The mind forms patterns that define for us our sense of reality. Mental models have been described as naturally occurring cognitive representations of reality, or the way in which reality is codified in our brain based on our understanding of reality. These representations of perceived reality give us our framework for cause and effect, lead us to expect certain results, give meanings to events, and predispose us to behave in certain ways. Our mental models become the basis for our perception, analysis, understanding, and behavior toward the object in question.[11] We think and act through our mental models because groups of neurons associated with them are wired together and have formed a circuit in our brains, driving our responses to everything we experience. Although mental models provide internal stability in a world of continuous change, they also blind us to facts and ideas that challenge or defy our deeply held beliefs. They are, by their very nature, fuzzy and imprecise. And everyone has a different model for even the simplest concept.

We have mental models for every role that we play: mother, daughter, sister, brother, father, son, coworker, boss, employee, et cetera. In addition, societies have adopted collective mental models about the way things ought to be. There are societal mental models about the roles of men and women: how men should behave and how women should behave. These models are reinforced over time through the media, peer pressure, and societal rewards. We have been taught through others, including parents and teachers, how to think and act, what to like, what to want, and how to value ourselves. Many of us adopted these notions without thinking about them, and they became hardwired in our neural net. For example, in my generation, the role of women was defined by June Cleaver, the wife and mother in the 1950s and 1960s TV program *Leave It to Beaver*. Women were supposed to take care of the home and the children, and to look very attractive doing it. We often saw June adorned with pearls as she cooked dinner. Men also have a very powerful societal mental model that they confront. Did you know that all men, if they are truly a man's man, have to be handy around the house? They have to know how to fix *everything*. Many men I know admit that they are not handy at all, and would much rather hire a contractor than pick up a hammer. This means that we can choose to adopt societal mental models or choose to create new mental models that serve us better.

In her book *Mindfulness*, Ellen J. Langer talks about a "state or trait that is common to all of us, namely mindlessness," which she defines as the human tendency to operate on autopilot, whether by stereotyping or simply by not paying attention.[12] Langer's research reveals that mindlessness results from automatic and habitual patterns of behavior.[13] The challenge is that these automatic responses discourage us from thinking about all of our options and new ways of responding. Because we are so accustomed to our mind's hardwiring, we often accept information uncritically, without noticing that the implications may not be valid when the context changes. Langer discusses how "premature cognitive commitments" can limit our options and our ability to see potential.[14] In this case, the mindless person is committed to one predetermined use of information, and other possible uses or applications are not explored. As we have seen, for situations that we experience repetitively, our brain locks us into mindless interpretations and responses to situations, and we often respond less than objectively.

Cognitive scientists are finding that people's mental models, which include their theories, expectations, and attitudes, play a more central role in human perception than was previously understood. People tend to experience what they expect to experience. The fact that our expectations, whether conscious or buried in our deeper brain centers, can play such a large role in perception has significant implications. What is hardwired in our neural net can become our experience. What we fundamentally believe about ourselves, what we believe to be true, what we have decided is important to us, what we focus on, is what our experience will be.

Here is how this played out for me one day. It was 2003; my Mitsubishi Galant had 168,000 miles on it, and I was about to move to Boston, so I needed a new car. I called my brother Hugh and asked him what kind of car I should buy. He told me the best deal was the new Lincoln LS. I said good; I liked the promotional offer of $0 down, 0 percent interest, and $0 due at signing. I went online and looked at the car. Then I went to the dealer to take a test drive and decided to think about it a few days. All of a sudden, everywhere I looked, I saw a Lincoln LS, in the same silver color. Has anything like this ever happened to you? The question is: Were the cars always there, or did they miraculously appear and follow me everywhere I went? Obviously, the cars were always there, but I didn't notice them before, not until I told my brain that the silver Lincoln LS was important to me. My brain brought to my attention what I wanted and considered important. This is a simple example of the power of our minds and our mental models. What we believe, and how we frame our world, ultimately determines how we will experience it.

Most of our mental models serve us well. But we all have a few that do not. If you are experiencing consistent problems at work or in your personal relationships, you may have a mental model that you are unaware of, which causes you to respond in ways that are inconsistent with your conscious objectives. The good news is, mental models can be changed. What doesn't fire together is no longer wired together. Every time we interrupt an automatic response, bring it to conscious awareness, and choose a different response, the nerve cells that are connected to each other start breaking their long-term relationship with each other and begin to create new neural connections. We will talk about the process of transforming mental models later in the book.

THE MIND AND THOUGHTS

Are you your thoughts? If your answer is yes, then which thought are you? Are you the thought you had when you woke up this morning, or the one you had around 2 p.m.? Or perhaps you are the final thought you have before you go to bed each night. Here is a hint: if you go back to the section about the subject-object relationship, the key takeaway was that anything that you can perceive through your senses or that you are aware of is an object to you, and therefore *not* you. Do you know the content of your thoughts? Do you sometimes say, "Well, that is the most ridiculous thought I've ever had"? Do you judge whether a thought is a good thought or a bad thought? The answer, of course, is yes. So, if we use our logic, we can conclude that we are *not* our thoughts. Our thoughts are certainly part of us, but we are *not* our thoughts. Have you ever woken up in the morning and said to yourself, "I am not going to think today, I am too tired"? No, of course not. Just as breathing happens and is constant, thoughts happen, and they are also constant.

We know now that thoughts, ideas, memories, and mental models are wired together in our neural net. Because of this, our thoughts tend to reinforce our existing mental models, and vice versa. For example, many women still have a mental model that tells them there is a glass ceiling in corporate America. Some believe that, despite a few exceptions to the rule, a corporate woman can't ascend past the level of vice president. If a woman vice president with this mental model learns that there is a senior vice president position available for which she is eminently qualified, what will her thoughts be? She may tell herself, "Oh, I shouldn't apply for that job; they have already decided to give it to a guy. They might even interview me, but in the end they are going to give it to a man and make up some excuse. I shouldn't even inquire about it, because everyone will just think I am crazy for applying." If she tries to resist these thoughts, her mind will come up with anecdotal data to support her mental model. She might even go online and find some compelling statistical data that supports her mental model, and after hours of exhausting thoughts, she will decide not to bother. This is the way mental models and thoughts often work. It is a mutually perpetuating and reinforcing system that can keep us locked into old ways of thinking and responding. Our minds rely on familiar, comfortable patterns, which limit our ability to respond objectively.

In addition to supporting our mental models, thoughts themselves have a significant impact on our lives, moment to moment, every day. Have you noticed that the content of many of your thoughts is self-judgment, negativity, and anticipating the worst? Sometimes these thoughts can be very limiting, unproductive, even harsh. There are times when we are just not very kind to ourselves. The problem with our negative thoughts is that the latest science has revealed that thoughts are very powerful, even impacting us physically. In his book *Change your Brain, Change Your Life*, Daniel G. Amen points out that "every thought sends electrical signals throughout your brain. Yes, they have substance, actual physical proper-ties, and they can impact every cell in our body, making us feel either good or bad."[15] Brain imaging clearly shows that when our minds are bur-dened with many negative thoughts, we tend to feel irritable, moody, or even depressed. Have you ever stopped to notice how you feel when you are mentally beating yourself up? Amen goes on to say that even though our thoughts are real, they are often wrong. Our thoughts lie. If thoughts often support our mental models, and if in some cases our mental mod-els are wrong, meaning unproductive and no longer serving us, then of course some of our thoughts will also be wrong. In essence the lies we sometimes tell ourselves are causing us emotional and physical harm.

It is important to remember that a thought is harmless unless we believe it. Byron Katie, in her book entitled *Loving What Is: Four Questions That Can Change Your Life*, proposes that "it is not our thoughts, but the attachment to our thoughts, that causes suffering."[16] As the Subject, since thoughts are an object of your awareness, you have the power to chal-lenge every thought. You can decide if you want to make that thought real. You can decide if you want to pay attention to that thought, change the thought, or ignore it. Amen suggests that when automatic negative thoughts pop up and you start feeling powerless or out of control, just talk back to the thoughts with attitude. Just like you can choose between juice or soda, you can talk back with attitude to a thought of "I always screw up" and choose to believe instead a thought of "when I focus on just doing my best, things normally turn out well." You choose. You are the Subject.

An important question for you to explore is, what mental model could be hardwired in my neural net that is connected to and reinforced by judgmental, negative, and unkind thoughts about myself?

THE MIND AND FEARS

New discoveries about the brain have also shed light on how much past experience, and the desire to avoid pain, shape our brain pathways. Richard Hanson and Richard Mendius, authors of *Buddha's Brain*, describe it this way: "Our brains are like Velcro for negative experiences and Teflon for positive ones. We automatically scan our worlds for past mistakes we dare not repeat, and future threats that we try desperately to avoid or prepare to face. Our brains were designed first and foremost to help us survive and pass on our genes, and thus they have automatic negative biases toward danger. When something happens that we don't like, our brains flag it as negative and store it for future reference."[17]

Fear is the emotion we feel when we sense danger. It is a protective emotion. Fear includes physical, mental, and behavioral reactions, and these are often tied to mental models. Because of our instinct for survival, the human brain has evolved a particularly strong capacity for detecting what neuroscientists call errors—perceived differences between expectation and reality. These error signals are generated by a part of the brain called the orbital frontal cortex. It is closely connected to the brain's fear circuitry, which resides in a structure called the amygdala. One of the amygdala's main functions is to protect us from threats or anything that might affect our well-being. It generates feelings and sensations of fear such as rapid heartbeat, sweaty palms, and muscle tightness. "When a person is in a condition of low to moderate stress, the prefrontal cortex calms the amygdala down and considers the pros and cons of the intended behavior."[18]

So, the prefrontal cortex actually helps you be more objective. It helps you think before you respond. With extreme stimulus, however, the activation of the amygdala shuts off the prefrontal cortex function, which is where conscious control and decision-making processes occur. Thus, when the amygdala perceives a stimulus as a threat, the conscious part of the brain automatically gets turned off. This is when we feel like we have "lost our minds." Neuroscientists call it the "amygdala hijack," because the subsequent response is controlled purely by the amygdala. In *Emotional Intelligence*, Daniel Goleman describes it as sudden and overwhelming fear or anger. When these parts of the brain are activated, they draw metabolic energy away from the prefrontal region that promotes and supports higher intellectual functions.[19] Error detection can therefore push people to become emotional and act more impulsively, less objectively. In the case of Jim and Scott at work, Jim was in the throes of an amygdala hijack, fueled by the spiraling of his negative thoughts, which is why he ran into his boss's office and confronted him about something that only existed in his own mind.

The bottom line is that we all experience fear. Are you aware of your fears? Do you know when you are feeling fearful? You are the Subject, aware of feeling fearful. This means that you are not your fears. The challenge is that fears often color our interpretation of "what is." For example, if we fear something, the sensations received through our senses, our objective means of knowledge, will be filtered through these fears by the mind. Our actions then become a reaction to a fear, rather than to "what is."

Some common fears my students have expressed in classes and workshops include:

1. **Fear of Failure**. My self-concept is tied to achieving goals and controlling outcomes. No one will like me or love me if I fail. I feel like a fraud. I fear that someone will find out that I'm not that smart.

2. **Fear of Success**. I feel that I am unworthy of happiness or success. I am afraid that if I succeed or accomplish my goal I will lose it once I have it.

3. **Fear of Death**. I am afraid of my own death and the death of my loved ones.

4. **Fear of the Unknown**. I have a fear of not being in control. I am afraid of what I don't know, I am afraid of what might happen.

5. **Fear of Isolation, Loneliness**. I fear not being liked or being rejected by everyone. I fear being alone.

The good news is that once we are consciously aware of our mental models, we can often reduce our fear, avoid the amygdala hijack, and respond more objectively.

LESSON LEARNED

Many times throughout my fruit juice venture I was fearful. The knot in my stomach that often flared was my signal for danger. I was often caught up in the amygdala hijack. What was I most afraid of? I must admit that the common fear coloring my response was my fear of failure. Perhaps if my fear of failure had not been driving my reactions, I might have been more objective, seen the obvious, and not spent six weeks in South Africa fighting for my business.

THE MIND, HABITS, AND TENDENCIES

Just like our thoughts will support our mental models, our minds have patterned and hardwired habitual responses and tendencies to support our mental models. For example, some people stand and fight when threatened, while others retreat or run away. "Fight or flight" is a routine tendency in response to fear generated by the basal ganglia. As we have seen, this is the part of the brain that patterns automatic thoughts and actions. This is why we find ourselves repeatedly responding the same way to the same situation. And at that moment, we don't feel that we can do anything about it. Once we recognize our mental models and identify those that may not be serving us, we can develop complimentary habits and tendencies to support our new ways of thinking and acting on our environment.

THE MIND AND INTUITION

The topic of intuition always comes up in my classes. Participants invariably want to know if intuition is objective or subjective. And most important, if intuition or gut feelings can be trusted. Here is what I have learned. There continues to be a debate among neuroscientists and psychologists about the origin and validity of intuition. From a neuroscientific perspective, intuition is defined "as implicit or unconscious recognition memory, to reflect the fact that intuition arises from information or sensory input that we receive and process without our conscious awareness which can subsequently be retrieved."[20] We all have an inner picture book of stored experiences based on what has happened to us previously in life. We also remember the outcome; did it end well or badly? Antonio Damasio of the University of Iowa College of Medicine suggests that with the aid of the entromedial prefrontal cortex, the part of the system that stores information about past rewards and punishments, we unconsciously assess the situation at hand and predict an outcome that often triggers the physiological response that people register as intuition or a gut feeling.[21] Just like mental models are often beneath our conscious awareness, our unconscious memory processes are collecting and storing data and nudging our responses to people and situations before we know what is going on. From this and my own experience, I believe that intuition can be a powerful tool if we learn to develop it and trust it. In the meantime, we know that just as our mental models, thoughts, and fears can be wrong and can motivate a response that we may regret, our intuition can also lead us astray. Being aware of our intuitive responses and evaluating them before we respond is critical to increasing objectivity.

YOU CAN'T BE MAD AT YOUR MIND

We often feel regret and get mad at ourselves when we look back over situations and see that we overreacted or responded in a way that was less than objective. It may be liberating to know now that you are not the only one; many people are doing the same thing and feel as you do. You can't be mad at yourself or your mind for unconsciously hardwiring your neural net since childhood, based on what the world looked like to you, what the media promoted, and what society seemed to value and reward. The wonderful thing is that our brains have the ability to reorganize themselves by forming new neural connections throughout our lives. This ability is called neuroplasticity. Sharon Begley, in her book *Train Your Mind, Change Your Brain*, describes neuroplasticity this way: "In response to the actions and experiences, a brain forges strong connections in circuits that underlie one behavior or thought and weakens the connection in others. Most of this happens because of what we do and what we experience of the outside world. In this sense, the very structure of the brain, the relative size of different regions, the strength of connections between one area and another, reflect the lives we have led . . . this mild sculpting can occur with no input from the outside world. That is, the brain can change as a result of the thoughts we have thought."[22]

Because of the power of neuroplasticity, you can, in fact, reframe your world and rewire your brain so that you are more objective. You have the power to see things as they are so that you can respond thoughtfully, deliberately, and effectively to everything you experience.

Now that we have a basic understanding of the neuroscience behind our cognitive errors and the capacity of the brain to change, we will focus on making this information actionable—teaching you *how* to increase your objectivity. Exercise 2 in your Action Plan will help you identify your mental models—those that may be serving you and those that are not.

ACTION PLAN: EXERCISE 2

WHAT DO YOU FUNDAMENTALLY BELIEVE ABOUT YOURSELF?

How you frame your world is directly related to what you think about yourself. Often, our self-concept or what we think about ourselves is a combination of what we think and what we think others think. Therefore, jot down:

- What you think about yourself, for example, *I am smart, I am hardworking, I am friendly*...
- Write down what you think others think of you.
- Notice the difference between what you think and what they think. Why do you think there is a difference?

Your thoughts shape who you are and how you feel and often support underlying mental models. Think about and be aware of your thoughts. Jot down:

- The content of your stream of thoughts.
- Are your thoughts supportive, or neutral, or unsupportive?
- If some of your thoughts are judgmental or harsh, what do you say to yourself?
- What could be an underlying mental model or belief for that thought?
- Is it true?

FEAR

- What you are afraid of?
- What are the mental models or underlying assumptions that make you fear it?
- What do you want or expect to happen?
- What do you think will happen if what you want or expect doesn't happen?

Part III

FRAMEWORK FOR OBJECTIVE LEADERSHIP

Chapter 4

OBJECTIVE DECISION MAKING

Are you surprised to learn how powerful your mind is? You now know that what you perceive, believe, and expect impacts your ability to evaluate situations clearly, make good decisions, and take effective action. As the Subject, you also know that you can choose your responses to everything you experience. Operating unconsciously and automatically, through mental models that you're not even aware of, can be limiting, unproductive, and sometimes destructive. Now you can learn to be conscious, deliberate, and effective in response to all the challenges and opportunities you confront each day.

The framework for objectivity on page 76 helps leaders develop their objectivity as a core competency for greater effectiveness.

The Objective Decision-Making Process is designed to be practical, to guide you through a process of understanding your own frame of reference and the perspective of others when evaluating situations, making decisions, and taking action. This is a process that is most effective in situations when you, the leader, have the time to gather and analyze various

Framework for Objectivity

Objectivity in the Moment	The Objective Decision-Making Process	Objectivity Long Term
◆ Mindfulness ◆ Creates Distance and Space ◆ Reverses Your Tendency	**THE OBJECTIVE LEADER** □ **Gathers and Accepts** the facts about the situation □ **Identifies** the mental models, emotions, and intuitions that may influence your conclusions □ **Evaluates** the underlying assumptions and determines validity and usefulness □ **Develops** new ways of thinking □ **Chooses** an objective response, taking into account all the possible consequences □ **Takes effective action** Mental Models, Thoughts, Fears, Tendencies	◆ Transformational Learning ◆ Cognitive Restructuring ◆ Attention Density

data points. However, there are also situations that come up quickly when you do not have the luxury of time to engage in a step-by-step process to increase your decision-making effectiveness. For this reason, the second component of the framework on the left side of the chart focuses on increasing objectivity in the moment, when things are happening fast, and there is intense pressure to respond quickly and effectively. While you are gaining control over your tendency to overreact in stressful situations and you are seeing things more clearly, it is also important for you to identify and shift those mental models that prompt your overreactions in the first place. Therefore the third component of the framework on the right side of the chart is focused on helping you create powerful new mental models that can frame a more successful and happier experience of your world.

In this chapter, I will walk through each step of the objective decision-making process and provide key questions for you to ask yourself along the way.

STEP 1. GATHER AND ACCEPT THE FACTS ABOUT A SITUATION.

When you are confronted with a situation in which a decision needs to be made, the first step is to gather all the facts. You must ask yourself, *What do I know about the situation? How can I be certain that I have all the information I need to make this decision?* As we have seen, our mental models and expectations often keep us trapped, and we avoid looking at all the facts about a situation. For example, we might only look at one aspect of the data, oftentimes the negative aspect, and dismiss everything else that might be relevant. This cognitive error is called selective abstraction.[1] For example, when reviewing the data from focus groups, Suzanne, a marketing research manager, only focused on the few negative comments indicating a lack of interest in the product, and concluded that the product should not move forward in the product development process. She ignored other data that indicated a willingness to pay at a lower price and dismissed data suggesting opportunities to improve the product. Given the number of products in the pipeline, no one questioned her recommendation. In this case, although it is not clear, the company could have lost an opportunity to be first to market with an innovative new product.

To understand the situation from all angles, it is important to gather information and perspectives from other team members and, when appropriate, from cross-functional areas within the organization. The other team members or areas will most likely see the situation through a different lens, and their perspectives may be very valuable and can help you arrive at a more objective conclusion. In the case of Suzanne, the marketing research manager, it might have been helpful to share the results of the focus groups with other members of the product development group, such as the design team and perhaps the data analytics team regarding competitive pricing, before making a no-go recommendation.

Once you have gathered all the relevant data, it is critical that you accept the facts about the situation. However, there are times when we simply do not want to see things as they are, and we futilely try to force change. As we have seen, the 2013 government shutdown was a perfect example of lack of acceptance and trying to force change. Frankly, I think that is why I stayed in South Africa so long. I could not accept the situation, so I figured that if I refused to leave, they would have to deal with me. Of course, they finally did, but not in the way that I had hoped.

Being an objective leader means accepting the reality of every situation. Trust me, denial and avoidance will only lead to poor decision making and ineffective action that could ultimately result in even worse consequences.

STEP 2. IDENTIFY THE MENTAL MODEL, EMOTION, OR GUT INSTINCT THAT MAY BE INFLUENCING YOUR CONCLUSIONS.

Once you have the data, you may find that you have an emotional response to it. If your first feeling is anger, frustration, or fear, it could be a sign that you may not be able to be objective. It is important to ask yourself, *What assumptions am I making that are causing me to feel angry, frustrated, or fearful about this situation? Do I have past experience with this?*

When confronted with a problem or situation, we sometimes blow things out of proportion. This is a cognitive error called catastrophizing—thinking that the absolute worst in a situation will happen without taking into account the possibility of other outcomes.[2] It is important to ask yourself, *What do I think will happen if this doesn't go exactly as planned?* For example, Joseph, a senior project manager, shared that he often attaches too much meaning to each and every project, assignment, or situation. He feels that his job could be at risk if he doesn't perform well. His fear of failure sometimes overtakes him to the point that some days he feels stuck or even paralyzed.

In addition to identifying any emotions that may be clouding your perspective of the situation, it is also important to acknowledge any gut feeling or intuition you might have about the situation. Malcolm Gladwell, in his best-selling book entitled *Blink*, strongly supports the power of intuition, which he also calls rapid cognition. In his book, he rallies behind the power and effectiveness of instinct, gut feelings, and snap judgments. According to his research, Gladwell has concluded that decisions based on intuition fared better than resolutions that relied on rational analysis. He emphasized that overthinking things can lead to a wrong decision—one far away from an individual's gut feeling. On the other hand, leading psychologists such as Nobel Prize winner Daniel Kahneman and others think that while intuition enables one to make choices without wasting time and effort, it is can lead to wrong decisions. While the scientists are debating the origin and validity of intuition, leaders should not discount their emotions or intuitive responses to situations. Rather they should consider them valuable data points to analyze and evaluate. The key point to remember is that your mind will perceive the data through the lens of your mental models, cognitive distortions, emotions, and gut feelings, so it is important that you take the time to reflect on what might be coloring your perceptions before you engage others in the decision-making process. Remember, once you become aware of them you can choose to be influenced by them or not. You are the Subject.

STEP 3. EVALUATE THE UNDERLYING ASSUMPTIONS AND DETERMINE THEIR VALIDITY OR USEFULNESS.

Once you have a handle on your cognitive appraisal of the situation and have identified your assumptions, thoughts, underlying emotions, and gut feelings about the situation, the next step is to evaluate them. Write them down, create a list. Your job now is to evaluate the validity or usefulness of each of your assumptions. It is important to remember that your thoughts are often tied to your mental models, so the first step is to jot down the negative thoughts and evaluate them as either useful or invalid and not useful. How? As the Subject, *you* can choose how to think about a situation. The first step is to challenge each and every negative or distracting thought by asking yourself if it is really true, or likely.[3] Often you will conclude that the thought or assumption is not true, or is very unlikely, and you can move forward. If not, then you'll need someone on your team or in your network who can help you be more objective. There is no shame in that. Until you transform the hardwired mental models that skew your vision of reality, sometimes it is difficult to challenge those thoughts on your own. (We will walk through that process later.) In the meantime, when you know that you cannot be objective about a situation, just like when you know you cannot install those kitchen cabinets yourself, find a resource and use it! A great resource could be someone close to you whom you trust, who knows you really well, who accepts you as you are, and does not want to change you. For me it is my twin sister.

You will notice when you create your list of assumptions that some are based on your prior experience with a similar situation. This can be good or bad. It is good when you are able to see the similarities and differences between the situations. It is good when you are able to see when the context may have changed. It is good when you learn from the past experience and draw insight and perspective from it as a data point only, not as a decision point. Where prior experience goes bad is when we quickly, without analysis, conclude, "Oh, we can do it this way, I've done it before and it worked." Instead ask yourself, *Would what I did last time be effective in this situation? Why or why not?*

STEP 4. DEVELOP NEW WAYS OF THINKING AND DEFINE GOALS.

Once you have identified and determined the usefulness and validity of your assumptions, the next step is to brainstorm new ways of thinking about the situation. It is important to engage this process nonjudgmentally, otherwise you will stifle creativity and innovative thought. Opening your mind to new ways of thinking without the distortion of mental models and past experiences will allow you to approach the situation more objectively. You will be able to draw conclusions about the objective reality of the situation based on valid and useful operating assumptions or hypotheses. The next step is to set goals. Ask yourself, *Based on what we now know, what is our desired result? What are the correct criteria upon which we will judge that we have achieved the required outcome?*

STEP 5. CHOOSE AN OBJECTIVE RESPONSE, TAKING INTO ACCOUNT ALL THE POSSIBLE CONSEQUENCES.

Choosing the most effective response now is easier because your judgment about the situation is sound, and the desired outcome is clearly defined and articulated. From the output of the brainstorming session, you can evaluate possible responses against the objective criteria established. You may ask, *Which response or approach will give us the best result based on our criteria?* For each option you are evaluating, think through all the possible consequences. Make the decision.

STEP 6. TAKE EFFECTIVE ACTION.

Once the decision is made, but before you execute, some leaders find that in order to gain buy-in and support, it is helpful to communicate their objective process to key stakeholders. The conversation should be concise, nondefensive, and collaborative, as follows:

- This is the data we analyzed.
- These are the additional input and perspectives we received.
- These were our initial assumptions that we validated, and these were the ones that we did not find useful.
- We brainstormed new ways of thinking about the situation and arrived at the following conclusions and operating assumptions.
- From there we determined the best outcomes and identified objective evaluation criteria.
- Measuring all the options against our criteria, we have chosen this approach.

Obviously, there will be times when you cannot engage this entire process with your team. The most important thing is to always ask *yourself* questions, to challenge your thoughts and underlying assumptions so that you are evaluating situations clearly and making effective decisions.

The exercise at the end of this chapter is for you to use the framework with one of the situations you remembered and described in the first exercise, a situation in which you were less than objective. While the Objective Decision-Making Process is essential in helping you make better decisions in real time, it is also a very helpful tool after the fact. It helps you think through situations to learn how you could have been more objective and gives you insight into your mental models and thoughts. Reflection is the key. The importance of reflection was cited in the Center for Creative Leadership's study, which investigated how managers and executives learn from their experiences. Reference is made to the current fast-paced and demanding managerial work environment, which leaves little time for managers to reflect on the actions they took when faced with a challenge. It is in these high-pressure situations that managers rely on what they know and what has led to success in the past. When the situation works out well, it reinforces the managers' old mental models. When things don't turn out well, there is often little time taken to reflect on the underlying assumptions, behaviors, and resulting decisions. Regardless of whether the situation turns out well or not, taking the time to reflect on your underlying assumptions, behaviors, and resulting decisions will help you determine if you have the most effective leadership mental models in place.

To help prepare you for that 20–20 hindsight exercise, it is important to see how easily the framework can be applied to even the simplest of situations: our extreme cases of subjectivity. Because you already have some level of objectivity—the situations do not involve you—it should be easy for you to apply the framework, see things clearly, and choose a more objective response.

CASE NO. 1: JIM AND SCOTT

OBJECTIVE DECISION-MAKING PROCESS

Gather and accept the facts.	What are the facts about this situation? What do I really know?	The boss, Scott, did not say hello to Jim as usual; he only nodded.
Identify the mental models, emotions or intuition that may influence your conclusions.	What are my assumptions, past experiences, or mental models that are influencing my conclusions?	Jim took Scott's behavior personally and overreacted out of fear. He assumed there were going to be layoffs. Jim magnified Scott's change in behavior as meaning the worst possible situation.
Evaluate the underlying assumptions and determine their validity or usefulness.	What is the validity or usefulness of these assumptions? What about my past experience can I use as a data point that will be useful?	Jim could not know what was going on with Scott; his assumptions were not valid or useful. Although Jim had been laid off before, he could not conclude that he would get laid off simply because the boss didn't say hello.
Develop new ways of thinking.	What is a different way of thinking? What are new conclusions about the situation? What are our operating assumptions that can be validated and are useful? What are our goals, and what are the evaluation criteria?	Jim could have thought that Scott's behavior had nothing to do with him. He could think of situations where he was distracted and changed his behavior and it only meant that he was distracted. Jim does want to maintain his good reputation and the relationship with his boss.
Choose an objective response or approach.	What is an objective response/approach, and what are the potential consequences?	Jim could do nothing at all, forget about it, and move on. Jim could ask Scott if he is okay the next time he sees him (which could annoy Scott.) Jim could run into Scott's office and only ask if he is okay and if he needs anything. Scott could perceive Jim as needing too much attention.
Take effective action.	If appropriate, communicate process.	Do nothing is the best alternative.

Epilogue: Scott had just learned that his 20-year-old daughter had just been injured in a car accident. He was too preoccupied to give Jim his usual boisterous greeting. When Jim came into his office, Scott looked at him in disappointment. The relationship changed from that day on because Scott now perceived Jim as insecure and impetuous.

CASE NO. 2: PATRICIA AND SAM

OBJECTIVE DECISION-MAKING PROCESS

Analyze and accept the facts.	What are the facts about this situation? What do I really know?	Sam called Patricia late and didn't say "I love you."
Identify the mental models, emotions, or intuitions that may influence your conclusions.	What are my assumptions, past experiences, or mental models that are influencing my conclusions?	Patricia had been hurt in relationships in the past and was overly sensitive. She found it difficult to trust her partner as a result.
Evaluate the underlying assumptions, and determine their validity or usefulness.	What is the validity or usefulness of these assumptions? What about my past experience can I use as a data point?	Projecting past experiences onto current situations is not seeing things clearly. Just because Sam didn't call on time does not mean he is cheating on her like her prior partner.
Develop new ways of thinking.	What is a different way of thinking? What are new conclusions about the situation? What are our operating assumptions that can be validated and are useful? What are our goals, and what are the evaluation criteria?	Patricia could give Sam the benefit of the doubt and give him time to communicate. Instead of thinking the worst, is it possible that he could have called late because he was going to surprise her with flowers? Patricia cares for Sam and wants to continue the relationship.
Choose an objective response or approach.	What is an objective response/approach, and what are the potential consequences?	Wait until after work to talk to Sam. Trust him, give him the benefit of the doubt.
Take effective action.	If appropriate, communicate process.	Do nothing, wait for Sam to get in touch.

Epilogue: In this case, Sam was late to work because of a flat tire and was disgusted with himself because he knew the tire was bald and had procrastinated for months about getting new tires. He called into work to tell his boss he would be delayed, but he didn't want to tell his new girlfriend how dumb he had been. This is the reason he waited to call. Even when he did call, he was still feeling silly and embarrassed, so he didn't stay on the phone long and forgot to say, "I love you." Sam had planned to call Patricia later to explain everything, but Patricia overreacted, assumed the worst, and thought she was protecting herself from hurt by calling him and breaking up with him.

Hindsight is 20–20, as they say. From your perspective, it was probably quite easy to think through the process and apply it to these extreme cases of subjectivity. However, when it is your situation, managing your inherent subjectivity can be a lot harder. The key is to take the time and engage each step of the objective decision-making process to increase your objectivity and overall effectiveness. In the next chapter we will focus on the second component of the framework: Objectivity in the Moment, how you can respond thoughtfully, deliberately, and effectively when things are happening fast.

ACTION PLAN: EXERCISE 3

Reflect on the situation that you described in Exercise 1 and complete the framework:

Analyze and accept the facts.	What are the facts about this situation? What do I really know?
Identify the mental models, emotions, or intuition that may influence your conclusions.	What are my assumptions, past experiences, or mental models that are influencing my conclusions?
Evaluate the underlying assumptions and determine their validity or usefulness.	What is the validity or usefulness of these assumptions? What about my past experience can I use as a data point?
Develop new ways of thinking.	What is a different way of thinking? What are new conclusions about the situation? What are my operating assumptions that can be validated and are useful? What are my goals, and what are the evaluation criteria?
Choose an objective response or approach.	What is an objective response/ approach, and what are the potential consequences?
Take effective action.	If appropriate, communicate process.

Chapter 5

OBJECTIVITY UNDER PRESSURE

When things are happening fast, when you are in the middle of a heated conversation with someone, when you are juggling multiple e-mails, and all of a sudden another one comes in that seems urgent, what do you do? In the moment, you do not have the time to stop and reflect on the mental model that may be coloring your view of the situation. You certainly do not have time to think through all the possible scenarios because you have to respond immediately.

The key is to create the space to respond appropriately even when you don't have time to reflect on what is going on. Most of us know when we are about to react emotionally. We can feel it. Often there is a brief warning before the amygdala hijack. For some of us, it is butterflies in the stomach; for some it is an increased heart rate; and for others it is a feeling of agitation. In that instant, before we respond, it is important to just *stop*, to say and do nothing. Do the exact opposite of what you are thinking. Trust what you have learned about the mind's automatic responses and be confident that if your mind is telling you to lash out, to push back...then you should just do the opposite. Tell the person that you will talk to them later, that now is *not* a good time to continue the conversation. If that is not possible, have a handy set of questions to create the space you need by asking the person to clarify what they are saying. For example: "It is important to me that I understand you correctly. Are you saying that...?" This may give you time to collect yourself before you respond, and it often gives the other person a reason to pause. If it is an e-mail that is triggering an emotional response, don't reply to the e-mail, or if you do, don't hit send. It is important to develop the mental space, the time to interrupt the spin in the mind at that moment, to avoid reacting inappropriately or in a manner that you may regret. It sounds simple, but while you are beginning the process of challenging your assumptions and questioning your mental models, this simple technique can help you to respond more objectively to "what is" in the moment. I have used this tactic many times; it really does work.

A funny example of this happened early on in my process to increase my objectivity, when I still had trouble creating the space to stop before responding. I had just been promoted to a new job, and I was doing the politically correct thing. I was making the rounds, introducing myself to the heads of all the departments, and having informal meetings with them to get their input on my new role and how best we could collaborate. One day, I received an e-mail late in the day from a colleague with whom I was scheduled to have lunch in two weeks. In the e-mail she publicly questioned what I had been doing so far and suggested what she thought my approach should be. She copied all of my peers and other members of the senior management team, including my boss, the president. I was outraged. *How dare she*, I thought to myself. I took it as a personal affront, although I knew based on my understanding of objectivity that there was indeed another way to look at it. But I was angry and I felt threatened. I wanted to respond to her e-mail with the same energy I was feeling from her, but I knew I couldn't do that. I had to do the opposite of what I was thinking, which was not to respond to the e-mail at that time. I knew that my response would surely be less than objective. So I went home and decided to go for a run to get it off my mind. Instead, with every step I was getting more and more angry. I came back, took a shower, got something to eat, and decided to watch a movie. Maybe the movie would distract me. It didn't. I wasn't watching the movie—I was thinking about the e-mail and kept looking over at my laptop, tempted to get up and send back a scathing e-mail. I knew this would be a mistake, so finally I drank half a glass of wine and took two aspirins and went to bed. I knocked myself out and it worked! I created the mental space that I needed so that I would not respond out of the anger I was feeling. I woke up the next morning, and over my cup of tea, I reread the e-mail and sent a carefully crafted response that was deliberate and effective (and of course hit "reply all," copying my peers and my boss). Naturally, I am not advocating drugs or alcohol to create the mental space needed to respond more objectively. There is a much better way.

A better tool is mindfulness. Jon Kabat-Zinn, a pioneer in the field of mindfulness, defines this as "the awareness cultivated by paying attention in a sustained or particular way, on purpose in the present moment, and non-judgmentally."[1] In other words, mindfulness is a way of paying attention to and clearly seeing and accepting what is happening in our lives. It helps us to be aware of and step away from our automatic and habitual reactions to our everyday experiences. Kabat-Zinn views mindfulness as "a core psychological process that can alter how we respond to the unavoidable difficulties in life. Mindfulness is not new; it is a part of what makes us human, namely the capacity to be fully conscious and aware."[2]

When we are fully conscious and aware, we actually know when we are about to overreact. When we are mindful, we have the mental space and are aware of when our moods change. When we are mindful, we can be aware of when our mental models are being challenged and when expectation does not meet with reality, which can trigger an emotional response. Remember that you are the Subject. Everything else is not you and is therefore an object of your knowledge or awareness. As we have seen, this includes your thoughts and your emotions. As the Subject, you have the inherent capacity to be aware of your thoughts and emotions, moment to moment, and you can choose your response to them. You merely need to develop that capacity.

Although it does take time, focus, and attention, you can gain mastery over your automatic responses. But we have to be conscious and aware to do it. We have to be mindful. The reality is that we are very rarely present in the moment. As Ellen Langer describes, too often we are on "automatic pilot, lost in memories of the past and fantasies of the future."[3] Even as you are reading this book, your mind has probably reflected back on an e-mail or a conversation you had earlier, or projected into the future about what you want to happen or don't want to happen tomorrow. Our minds are in one place but our bodies are in another. This is common to all of us. It is also the nature of the mind. "The brain produces simulations, mini-movies that take us out of the present moment. Have you ever found yourself sitting in a morning meeting, and all of a sudden your mind is a million miles away replaying a past event or thinking about what negative thing might happen in the future? Many of our movie clips are based on our fears and our mental models. Every time these mini-movies play, especially the negative clips, we strengthen the connections between the event we are replaying and the negative emotions that may be associated with it."[4] If our minds are only rarely present, how can we recognize when we are about to respond less than objectively? Just by becoming aware of what is occurring within and around us, we can begin to untangle ourselves from mental preoccupations and difficult emotions. Because the brain has been trained to work on automatic pilot, it does take a conscious decision and effort to pay attention to what's happening in the present.

To increase our objectivity, we must learn to switch off the mini-movies. Objectivity requires us to be mindful, present in the moment, and experiencing what is happening without judgment. The challenge is that we instantaneously and automatically judge situations and other people as well as our own thoughts, feelings, and behaviors. We react intensely to our experiences, particularly unwanted experiences, and to our initial responses to them. Sometimes we think things like, *What a bonehead, how could I do that, what was I thinking, I can't take this anymore.* Our minds spin and spin and spiral down to a place of self-judgment and often self-loathing. How can we respond objectively with all of this going on in our minds? Accepting rather than rejecting what is happening in the current moment does not mean believing or accepting that one can do nothing to prevent the situation from continuing or getting worse in the next moment. Nor does it mean accepting and allowing one's own automatic and habitual responses, no matter how compelling or justified such responses may initially feel. It is in fact just the opposite: accepting the current moment enables you to prevent the external situation, and your internal reactions to it, from robbing you of an opportunity for an effective response in the next moment.

The good news is that we *can* increase our mindfulness. We can develop our capacity to create distance between an automatic and instantaneous emotional response, recognize what is really going on, and respond more objectively. Just as we improve our physical fitness through regular physical exercise, we can develop mindfulness through deliberate mental practice. It means training the mind to be aware of what it is doing at all times, including being aware of when the mini-movie starts, being aware of what we are thinking when we think. The mental activity of mindfulness training activates specific regions of the brain and promotes feelings of well-being. There are two sets of techniques you can employ. One is formal mindfulness practice, where you set aside a period of time to practice mindfulness. This is also called meditation. The second technique doesn't require dedicated time. Jon Kabat-Zinn refers to these as informal mindfulness practice, or mindfulness in action techniques. In both techniques, the goal is to train your mind to stay present and not wander off. According to Hindu and Buddhist philosophy, meditation is about changing the focus of your mind, focusing on an object and bringing your mind back when it wanders. You may have heard about Vipassana meditation, a Buddhist technique for focusing on the breath. The breath lies at the intersection between the voluntary and involuntary nervous system. In this meditation, you simply sit quietly and focus your attention on the inflow and outflow of your breath. You do this without trying to control your breath, but just by being aware of it. When we let our attention settle on the breath and let the breath be, breathing calms down, and with it the mind.

Another mindfulness technique is called mindfulness of sounds.[5] While sitting quietly, listen to the sounds around you. Let go of naming and categorizing the origin and source of the sounds. If you notice your mind wandering, be aware for a moment of where your mind is going, and then gently bring your attention back to the sounds in the here and now.

If you don't have time to set aside, increasing mindfulness can be as simple as focusing your awareness on something physical that you do every day. For example, notice how tightly you hold the steering wheel when driving, or be aware of the music you hear when you are put on hold. You may also focus your awareness on the breath when a specified environmental cue occurs, such as waiting for the other person to answer the phone, waiting at a red traffic light, walking, listening to music, or getting dressed. Do you know what happens to your breathing or voice tone in an argument? Start being mindful of this. As the Subject, you can train your brain to be aware of everything that is happening within you, and can therefore choose a more objective response to challenging situations.

The key here is for you to find what works for you. Personally, I have found that focusing on my breath even for a few seconds really calms the spin in my mind. It also helps to focus my attention on being aware of my sense of touch. I either stay conscious of my feet touching the floor or, if I'm in a meeting, focus on my fingers touching each other. I practice being aware of what is going on around me while keeping the sense of touch in my awareness.

A very effective technique is "interrupting the spin." When you find yourself having an emotional response and you can't seem to shake it off, interrupt the spinning of the mind. One female executive reported that when she is frustrated and about to do or say something she might regret, she gets up from her desk and takes a short walk, or goes to get a cup of coffee. This has worked so well for her that she uses the "interrupt the spin" technique with her employees. When she perceives an employee behaving a bit defensively and resisting her input, she pauses and invites the employee to go get a cup of tea with her. Often, the employee's mood changes and a more productive conversation takes place. The mind can spin and spin. It can be uncomfortable, and as many people will admit, once it gets going it is hard to stop the spin. Something that happened at work on Friday and triggered your sense of insecurity can spin in your mind all weekend long. Being mindful so that you are aware when your mind is spinning, and then interrupting the spin, will help you be more objective in the moment. Being aware of your triggers so that you stop before responding is also critical. Exercise 3 will help you identify your triggers.

LESSON LEARNED

It is not enough to just be aware of your triggers. After you have stopped, reversed your tendency, and responded more objectively in the moment, it is also important to subsequently reflect on what is causing the response in order to ensure that you are seeing things clearly. For example, after my five-year exclusive distribution agreement was signed, and The Diplomat warned me to be careful, I was clearly aware of the knot in my stomach at that moment. I was definitely confused and afraid. Although it was correct to continue with the US product launch event at that moment, later I should have reflected on what I was truly afraid of and objectively evaluated all my options. A more objective response could have included identifying other unique international beverage products to sell into my rapidly developing distribution channel. I learned that our triggers can often provide us with an opportunity to reflect and make a better decision overall, beyond the present situation that triggered the emotion. Think of your triggers as valuable information!

ACTION PLAN: EXERCISE 4

To be objective in the moment requires being present in the moment so that you can be aware of your triggers. Triggers are physiological responses to what you experience. Triggers are the precursor to "losing your mind," the amygdala hijack. Jot down your triggers.

- How do you feel right before you get angry?
- How do you feel right before you get frustrated?
- How do you feel right before you cry?

Complete the list, and jot down how you feel right before any other emotion that you might feel before you respond less than objectively.

Chapter 6

CHANGING YOUR MIND

Identifying and Shifting Limiting Mental Models

Hopefully, by now, you are practicing being more objective in the moment and are creating the space you need so you don't send that scathing e-mail or speak dismissively to your coworkers. As a more objective leader, I hope that you're building in the time to question your underlying assumptions and develop new ways of thinking about the challenges you face each day.

In this chapter we will focus on the third component of our Framework for Objectivity: long-term objectivity. Though handling day-to-day interactions and projects more objectively will produce excellent results, becoming a truly objective leader requires that we identify and transform the limiting and unproductive mental models that are driving our ineffective responses in the first place. As a quick recap, our mental models frame our world and underlie many of our overreactions and automatic responses that we later regret. These mental models can keep us trapped in old ways of thinking and acting that often run contrary to our conscious objectives and cause us to get in our own way. So in this chapter, we will focus on transformation. The neuroplasticity of the brain gives us the opportunity to literally rewire our neural net with new ways of thinking that will increase our overall success *and* happiness.

Transformative learning is an effective process to combat limiting and unproductive mental models. Homer Johnson, who has done extensive research in mental models, defines transformative learning as "a process of critically reflecting on one's behavior and the assumptions underlying it, and developing new and more effective ways of understanding and acting upon the environment."[1] He asserts that mental models change through disorienting events that challenge the existing mental model. For instance, as we know, losing a million dollars can definitely drive a person to rethink things. While mindfulness helps us deal with the effects, transformative learning helps us deal with the root causes—the mental models that drove the initial reaction.

COMMON MENTAL MODELS

Because many mental models are subconscious, identifying them is challenging. A good way to start is to look at the most common mental models. In 2010, I collaborated with a Babson College MBA student and a professor of statistics at Babson on an internal research project to focus on the role mental models play in management, leadership, and decision making. Our hypothesis was that specific mental models do influence personal and professional behavior. Some are generally helpful, while others are not. We assumed that mental models that do not serve a person well can be shifted, or new ones acquired, through a series of activities, techniques, and tools. The goal of our research was to investigate the following questions:

- What mental models are most predominant in the workplace?
- Can mental models be shifted?

- Can they be shifted even if the person is unaware of having them?
- What usually precipitates a shift in a mental model?
- How do shifts in the mental model influence professional behaviors, i.e., management practices/leadership style?
- How do shifts in the mental model influence personal behaviors?
- How well does the Babson Objectivity Course help identify and shift limiting and productive mental models?

We conducted online surveys before and after the class, as well as hundreds of personal interviews and one-on-one sessions with students and workshop participants. Based on our findings, it appears there are several common mental models. Do any of these sound familiar to you?

EXTERNAL VALIDATION: I NEED OTHERS TO LIKE ME AND THINK I AM SMART.

If you are like most people, you care very much about what other people think about you. In our survey, 62.2 percent of people responded that their self-worth was strongly tied to what others think. What we tend to forget is that everyone is instantly judging, categorizing, and responding to everyone else based upon a myriad of influences *in their own mind*. Often we are being judged and responded to in ways that have nothing to do with us at all. Picture this: I walk by a tall woman wearing a gray dress. Instantly I feel that I don't like her, and I try to avoid her. Why? Because she reminds me of a teacher who called on me in third grade to recite the Emancipation Proclamation, and I froze. It was my most embarrassing moment, and that teacher's image is now indelibly imprinted on my mind. Every time I see a tall woman in a gray dress, my mind calls up that embarrassing moment, and now I have an initial negative response to anyone that reminds me of the teacher. Our minds respond instantaneously, in the present, based upon memories of things that happened in the past. Ask yourself: Can you afford to spend time worrying about what someone else's initial response to you may be, when it could have absolutely nothing to do with you? Most importantly, can you afford to allow any-one else's perception of you to shape how you feel about yourself?

Unfortunately, most of us can't help it. In their book *On Self and Social Organization*, social psychologists C. H. Cooley and Han-Joachim Schubert called this phenomenon the Looking-Glass-Self and summed it up as follows: "I am not what I think I am and I am not what you think I am; I am what I think that you think I am."[2] In many cases, we choose to associate with people whose opinions we value and respect—psychologists call this the "in-group"—and we seek approval and validation from them. The opinions of this in-group become the basis for how we value our-selves, for our self-acceptance. The problem, given what we now know, is that if you base your self-concept on what you think others think of you, then you will always be vulnerable. Your self-concept has no true founda-tion. If the other person is having a good day and responds to you in a friendly, affirming manner, then you feel good. If not, you wonder what you did wrong. We are constantly trying to project an image of ourselves based on what we think others want, but since we really don't know what they want, what we are really doing is deciding what we think they want and then trying to project that image. It's a losing game.

Take the case of Jonathan, a very astute white male in his early 30s who is a senior analyst in a financial services firm. Jonathan shared that it was dif-ficult for him to admit how much his happiness depended on other people's perceptions of him. What makes this common experience so insidious is that the same people from whom we are seeking validation are also seeking validation from us. It is how virtually all of us were socialized. Jonathan fur-ther describes his External Validation mental model this way: "I am always looking for validation from others, especially at work so that I know that I am doing things correctly and that I am on the right track. Without this approval from others, I automatically assume that people disapprove and I begin to question my actions and beliefs and become very insecure."

As we saw earlier, the problem with this is that the assumptions we make about what others think of us are often wrong. When we encounter unwanted or unexpected behavior in someone else, we think the person must be mad at us, so we should go and find out what we did to offend them.

Here is how Susan, a 40-year-old senior project manager for a global health-care company, describes this common experience:

> I was the project manager for a high-profile global project where my team and I were responsible for upgrading the communications infrastructure to better link our satellite offices in 32 countries around the world. All eyes were on my team. Consequently, I was under daily stress and pressure to maintain composure and to move the project along to completion. My manager was pretty hands-on and because of the high-profile nature of the project, I sent him e-mails at the end of each day with a status update so that he could update his boss. Because of this he always responded to all of my updates. This time I sent the update and status e-mail and I heard nothing. And I immediately began to panic. The following questions ran through my head: Is my manager disappointed in the outcome of this step? Did someone call my manager and tell him I screwed something up? Did I get the deadline wrong? Did I miss the deadline? Unfortunately, this is just what immediately went through my panicked mind. In the next few hours, my thoughts would get worse. I decided to go to my manager's office to see what was wrong. As I went to approach my manager's office, I came around the corner to the loud slam of his office door. I caught his glance right before the door slammed shut, and the look on this face was what I read to be a grimace. My level of fear hit a new high. *This is it,* I thought, *I'm doomed. I'll never get to complete this project and I'll never work on another project or survive the week at this company.* I instant-messaged a few of my colleagues around me, to see if they could offer some insight into what was going on. The responses were generally this: "I have no clue, he's in a terrible mood today, his door keeps being randomly slammed shut and we're all probably being laid off." I got

up from my desk; I couldn't take it anymore. If I had screwed up, he could at least tell me to my face. I knocked on his door. He opened it and he said "WHAT." I saw he was on the phone, he told me he'd call me into his office when he was off the phone. I closed the door as I left. *THIS IS IT*, I thought, *he is getting approval to get rid of me and it's going to happen in the next 20 minutes.* An hour later, after I'd been frozen in fear at my desk, he called me and asked me to come into his office. I put on my brave face or what I could muster up of it. I entered his office and sat down. Almost immediately he said, "Today has been a rough day. My wife had to take my daughter to the emergency room because my daughter's Crohn's disease is acting up. I'm leaving in an hour to meet them." My face sank, and I apologized for interrupting him earlier when his door was closed. He told me, "It's okay, don't take it personally if I close my door abruptly." He laughed a little, which was a bit of a relief, although I was concerned that he was laughing at me. Then he went on to compliment my completion of this recent milestone of the project. I was pleased about this, thanked him, and said that I'd be less quick to judge if I didn't hear his feedback as soon as possible.

I have heard countless stories just like this, of situations where I See, Therefore It Is, and then it turns out it *isn't*. In the best case, we lose a few hours of productivity and drive ourselves crazy, and in the worst case, we irreparably harm our reputation and career.

LESSON LEARNED

For me, this External Validation mental model played out a little differently. My self-concept was largely dependent on the role I played. You may remember from my story that first I was Miss American Express, and then later I became the Fruit Juice Lady. How I valued myself—and just as importantly, why I thought I was valued, appreciated, and in some cases loved by others—was dependent on the job I had, the role I played, the title I held. My self-concept was foundationless, built on a role that could change at any time. Because of this, I was always vulnerable. This meant I had to hold onto that role no matter what, and I needed others to validate this concept of myself. When I looked back on the faxes I sent to the South African Diplomat during my six weeks in South Africa, I felt embarrassed by how often I wrote that a person I had met was impressed with me. It is indeed possible that this need for external validation may have blinded me from effectively mitigating my supplier risk. The lens through which I framed my world was to hold onto the role at any cost, because otherwise, who would I be? Diversifying my product portfolio was a better business model, but perhaps, in my mind, it would not allow me to save South Africa. For social entrepreneurs, it is important that even though your social mission is compelling and rewarding, you must first have a sustainable business model.

COMPETITION: I CONSTANTLY COMPARE MYSELF WITH OTHERS TO DETERMINE MY VALUE.

Many of us do this and often end up feeling bad about ourselves. Our sense of value or worth is relative, based upon how well others are doing. Some people feel that everyone in their office is a competitor. They have to appear more intelligent and achieve greater results than everyone else in order to feel good about themselves. For some this plays out as a need to always be right. Some people will keep arguing, ad nauseum, trying to prove their point, even though their position is tenuous at best. The truth is many of us have been socialized to think that if we are not the very best, if we are not at the top 1 percent of whatever it is we do, then we are not good enough. To reinforce this already pervasive mental model, society has established a competitive hierarchy for just about everything.

Consider performance reviews. Many of us have learned the hard way that if we don't get an "exceeds expectations" rating or something higher than a 3 on a scale of 1 to 5, not only will we not get the highest bonus, but we may not get the next promotion—or even a raise. Many high school students are taught that if they don't have a 4.0 GPA, score in the 99th percentile on admissions tests, and demonstrate leadership in sports and participate in clubs, they won't get into college anywhere. If I work in a biotech research firm and everyone around me has a PhD and an MBA, but I have only the PhD, I am not good enough.

This competitive hierarchy is debilitating, and it starts very early. Here are two peoples' descriptions of how this particular mental model plays out for them.

Juan is a 30-something male from South America who was not able to follow the traditional education and career track of many of his peers. Although he is just as good or even better, in some cases, than most of his peers in the engineering industry, he still feels the impact of the Competitive mental model and expresses it this way: "I will do my best in life to achieve a better condition (earn more money) so I will not feel less than others anymore. The result of this is that I spend too much time working, not spending enough time with my family or taking care of my health."

Sue Ling, an Asian woman in her late 20s, always feels the pressure from her family and society to perform and talks about it this way: "Growing up in a culture where I was constantly being judged based not only on my own performance but also relative to that of others, I developed the habit of judging myself based on how others perform. I have also cultivated a biased view of good performance. I am not good enough unless other people say so. Based on these biases, I became addicted to external validation."

PERFECTIONIST: I HAVE TO BE PERFECT IN EVERYTHING I DO.

In a recent workshop with senior-level women leaders, one of the women raised her hand and said, "I have a Perfectionist mental model. Wanting to be perfect is a good mental model, right?" I replied, "How's that working for you?" She replied, "I am exhausted, my kids aren't speaking to me, my husband is about to leave me, and I am about to lose my job." I said, "Well then, apparently it's not working so well." She agreed. The salient question, however, is not whether your mental model is empirically good or bad; the question is always does the mental model serve you? It is unproductive to adopt a mental model that you think is good but that really doesn't work for you. The Perfectionist mental model clearly did not serve this particular woman well. Yet many of us struggle with it. Some people even put obstacles in front of themselves so that they can overcome them and prove that they are perfect. Even when they exceed their supervisors' or peers' expectations, they are still not satisfied; they set arbitrary goals for themselves and continually challenge themselves to excel. They keep moving the bar.

Carolyn, a savvy young woman in her mid-20s, in graduate school to pursue a career in finance, describes her Perfectionist model this way:

As long as I can remember, I always had a need to be perfect, perceived as flawless in the eyes of my friends and colleagues, my loved ones, and, most challengingly, myself. My perfectionist persona served as an umbrella that covered and guided my thoughts, actions, and goals in all aspects of my life: professional, personal, and social. I believe that my overarching need to be perfect has shaped who I am today, both for good and bad. . . . I strongly believe that my perfectionism, the manner in which I choose to conduct my everyday life, and my personal value have been the primary reason that I have achieved many of my life's goals thus far. Often my Perfectionist mental model results in my need to be able to "do it all"—complete all homework assignments, go out to dinner with friends, work out weekly at the gym, have a spic-and-span house, even if realistically there is not enough time in the day. Also, I often take much longer than others to accomplish tasks, since I associate taking more time to complete something with a phenomenal job. Any time that I successfully complete a task in a timely manner, I perceive that I didn't do my best. My Perfectionist mental model has also created a barrier to achieving a sense of personal contentment and joy. I often find myself caught up in the details rather than focusing on the big picture, emphasizing the bad rather than the good, and, more times than not, feeling apprehensive about the outcome of my actions rather than proud and satisfied.

This is how the model plays out for Walter, a man in his early 40s, happily married with two girls, and a well-respected, high-performing project manager for a very large engineering company.

As far as evaluating myself, I set a very high bar for myself in everything I do. At work, I work very hard and deliver results. I take pride in my work and always strive for continuous improvement. This is evident in the promotions and bonuses I receive. At home, I try to be the best father and husband that I can. Others notice how much of a family man I am and they admire it. The down side of being a perfectionist is twofold: I become defensive whenever anyone comments about my work, and my response is usually proportional to the degree I think they are trying to attack me. I take it personally when, in some cases, I should not. This certainly has raised some comments from my management about my overreactions to what they see as innocent comments from others. Another scenario where this plays out is related to my kids. To me, my kids are the best kids ever and they pretty much walk on water. I become subjective to any statements that paint my kids in a different light. I close my ears and refuse to accept any criticism of my kids. This has caused some tension with my wife, who is more objective in this respect. My Perfectionist mental model equates asking for help with weakness. This has caused me to be less compassionate than I should be, especially when it comes to my wife. Moreover, with a Perfectionist mental model, I sometimes judge others by my own standards. As a result, people often fall short of my expectations, and I become critical of them. I do recognize that this is not right, and that it is an effort for me to accept others for what they are.

Here is one more example. Roger, a highly intelligent and competitive single man in his early 30s, recently went back to school for his MBA while working for a start-up company. He describes his Perfectionist mental model this way:

> Another word that I use to describe myself, and that others have used to describe me, is perfectionist. This relates to my need for achievement, as I want to achieve at a high level. My own standard for a high level is often greater than the standard to which others— teachers, supervisors, family, peers—would hold me. But since hard work, intelligence, and achievement are part of my self-concept, I strive to fulfill my own sense of what it takes to uphold these virtues. A related variable is the degree to which I will take risks. I usually look toward a middle ground, not too little risk but not too much risk. Too little risk could result in accomplishments that I don't feel good enough about because the degree of difficulty was too low, while too much risk could result in paralysis because I don't want to embark on a project that could result in failure, or at least a failure to meet my own goal or the goal I perceive others have for me. At times, my tendency toward perfection borders on obsession, as I'll spend an inordinate amount of time thinking about a work or school project or an approach to an interpersonal situation, when it would probably be more effective if I just acted quickly and efficiently.

Although the drive to be a perfectionist is the overarching mental model, it is interesting to see how this one model can play out so differently in people. It is also important to note that a mental model can play out positively as well as negatively. Carolyn, for example, feels that her Perfectionist mental model is positive because she feels that it is what makes her successful and keeps her motivated and focused. On the other hand, she feels that her Perfectionist mental model is a barrier to her personal contentment and joy.

CONTROL: I MUST BE ABLE TO CONTROL MY ENVIRONMENT. MY SELF-CONCEPT IS BASED ON HOW WELL I CAN CONTROL PEOPLE AND OUTCOMES.

Many of us have a need to control. In our survey, 67 percent of respondents said they had a strong need to control, 44 percent said their self-worth was *often* connected to their ability to control circumstances, and 19 percent said that their sense of self-worth is *more often* connected to their ability to control circumstances. I was surprised that this wasn't even higher, considering how we have all been socialized. From our earliest years, we have been told that the result is what matters. Ellen Langer refers to this as "education for outcome" and proposes that it is one of the primary reasons we become mindless. "From kindergarten on, the focus of schooling is usually on goals themselves, rather than the process by which they are achieved. This single-minded pursuit of one outcome over another, from tying shoelaces to getting into Harvard, makes it difficult to have a mindful or objective attitude about life. When children start a new activity with an outcome orientation, questions of 'Can I do it?' or 'What if I can't do it?' are likely to predominate, creating an anxious preoccupation with success or failure rather than drawing on the child's natural, exuberant desire to explore."[3] This Control mental model plays out in many ways. Here are a few examples:

Sally, a single, very hardworking, and compassionate woman in her early 30s, works in a large nonprofit and describes it this way:

> In addition to my Perfectionist mental model, I have come to realize that my thoughts and actions are often determined by a Control mental model. As a means to achieve perfection, I convince myself that I am able to maintain complete control of myself, others, and all the objects

that play a role in my life at a particular point in time. Therefore, it logically makes sense that by following this Control mental model, I should be able to direct the outcomes of my actions as well as the actions of the people around me. Although I know deep down that this is not a realistic belief, my Perfectionist and Control mental models create a different illusion, and consequently I set myself up to fail.

Michael, an intense but very personable young entrepreneur in his late 20s, shares the following:

Control Freak. Micromanager. Can't let go. Takes things too personally. Stubborn. All of these are terms I would ascribe to myself when I take a hard look back at past work experiences, and I imagine others have thought the same. I seem to always want to be in control, or end up trying to be in control, in whatever situation I end up in. In many ways this has led me toward being a leader, but it is not without its downside. Because growing up, I often felt like I had no control over my life, in some ways I have overcorrected by always putting myself in situations where I can feel like I am in control. I don't even like being a passenger in the car if my wife is the one driving.

LESSON LEARNED

My need to control outcomes was dominant throughout my business venture. I was trying to force things to be what I wanted them to be. I wanted people to respond to me the way I wanted: for example, I wanted the other suppliers to agree with my marketing plan. Instead of accepting the fact that they had different points of view, I kept trying to convince them. I wanted the suppliers to see things the way I wanted and behave the way I wanted. Instead of trying to understand their points of view, their motivations, I kept trying to prove that my strategy, my approach was the best for all.

INSECURITY: I AM NOT GOOD ENOUGH—I CANNOT ACCEPT MYSELF AS I AM, I AM LIMITED.

One of the most powerful and pervasive mental models I have found in many people of all ages, walks of life, and career status—from presidents of corporations to high school interns—is this: *I believe, deep down, that I am not quite good enough, I am limited in some way, I am not 100 percent acceptable to myself. I can be better.* It is fascinating to see how readily and openly people admit this. This appears to be a fundamental mental model for many of us, and it underlies much of our negative spiral of thinking, the often harsh voice of judgment that many of us experience. This mental model becomes the basis for our self-concept. How often are you beating yourself up each day? How often are you worrying about what others *may* be thinking about you? We can be very hard on ourselves, and it may be because deep down, we don't feel good enough.

Here are a few examples of how this can play out.

Anika, an Indian woman in her late 20s whose parents immigrated to the United States when she was three, is a top-performing sales executive for a leading technology company. She describes her model this way:

> "I'm incompetent / not good enough" is a very strong mental model for me. When I was growing up, my dad was a little nervous and critical of me, wanting to make sure that I pursued the best path for myself so that I would grow up to be secure and self-sufficient. He meant well, but his constant criticism started the notion in the back of my mind that making mistakes was a really bad thing. This notion was reinforced many times over when I went to a small private school where the judgment and criticism was even worse. I left the school wary of making mistakes and created my own critical voice to ensure that I gave myself enough warning before I would screw up and something bad would happen. And that voice is very harsh!

Sharon, a very intelligent and highly capable woman in her late 30s, works in the research department of a medical devices company and links her "I am not good enough" with the External Validation and the Competitive mental models in this way:

> I believe I have the very common, potentially innate, mental model that "I am not good enough." I tend to constantly compare myself to everyone around me, so much that I am always finding people who are better than me at everything. This makes me feel uncomfortable with positive feedback because I do not believe the positive things that people say about me. This mental model creates a stream of negative thoughts; for example, when I receive a compliment (or any form of positive feedback), I immediately become uncomfortable. I find reasons to deny the comment in my mind, and my body language clearly shows my discomfort. Thoughts such as "He doesn't know the 'real' me" or "She's wrong because one time xyz happened" enter my mind. I have difficulty stopping the negative stream of thoughts that come flooding in.

Jarrod, a consultant from London in his late 30s who enrolled in a part-time MBA program, puts it this way:

> My dominant mental model is the thought/belief that I'm not good enough. It has mainly driven me to be subjective about certain situations in my professional life as a consultant. But it also happens to impact me outside my job, e.g., at school. In many of these situations, I felt fear of not meeting the expectations of my teams, supervisors, or teachers because I thought that I am not good enough. This usually has resulted in a mental state where I have been more focused on my fear of underperforming and the potential negative consequences rather than on my actual job/task. Basically, I have been making up a lot of stuff that wasn't really there. On the one hand, this has often resulted in unhappiness about my situation,

which made my job/life less enjoyable. Ironically, it has also hindered me from working as effectively as possible.

Why do so many of us suffer from this same mental model? After experiencing a disorienting event that only validated a nagging feeling of not being good enough, I began searching for a reason to change my mind about it. In doing so, I reviewed a number of theories that have been proposed by social psychologists, psychiatrists, religious leaders, and philosophers. The one that rang truest to me was the one espoused by Swami Dayananda Saraswati, renowned scholar of Sanskrit and the ancient philosophy known as Vedanta. He starts with the premise that we are all self-conscious, self-judging human beings, yet when we are infants, our only way of judging ourselves is through the eyes of our caregiver. We trust that person completely. They are like a God to us: all knowing, all powerful, all pervasive. Our survival depends on that Godlike person. If we are lucky, each day, the caregiver holds us, feeds us, bathes us, and plays with us. We feel safe, warm, and happy. As a child in the early stages of development, we need that caregiver in plain sight in order to feel that we are okay. Did your mother ever say to you, "You're okay, you're okay," when you wandered three feet outside of your direct line of sight to her? You responded with confidence and then went racing down the hall to explore something new. One day, however, that Godlike person inevitably, unwittingly betrays that trust, perhaps by not giving you the attention that you are used to. Perhaps they are late getting home, you are hungry, and they don't respond well to your cries. Or even worse, perhaps they are preoccupied and ignore you when they first walk in the door. How would a helpless infant react to this change? Still just developing their cognitive abilities, it is possible that they would feel that there must be something wrong with them because nothing could be wrong with "God," this all-knowing person upon whom they depend for their survival.

Many of us internalize this inevitable experience in our subconscious as evidence that we are not good enough. It then becomes indelibly imprinted in our vast neural net, strengthening each time we feel disappointed. Many children with this subconscious mental model constantly seek approval from their parents, and some become so dependent on the validation from caregivers that they never want to leave their side. Even as adults, many of us live the lives our parents want and expect from us because our parents' approval is the only basis for our self-worth. Others seek validation outside of the home from teachers, other children, and other adults. This need for validation often continues well into and throughout adulthood. This theory closely links to British psychiatrist John Bowlby's Attachment Theory, which espouses that the sense of emotional security or insecurity a child develops in the first years of life strongly shapes, over the entire life span, emotional stability, self-image, and attitudes toward others."[4]

The most interesting observation of the objectivity research has been the connection between the Insecurity: "I am not good enough" model and the other mental models of External Validation, Competition, Perfectionist, and Control. If we go back to our overarching theory about mental models—namely that what we believe is what we are going to experience, and that the mind constructs and reinforces mental models in our neural net—we find an interesting correlation. The hypothesis is that since many of us know how unpleasant it feels to believe that we are not good enough, in response, we try to develop other mental models, beliefs, and behaviors to compensate. A few examples of this include:

- I am going to be a perfectionist so that I will be good enough.
- I cannot ask for help because help means I am weak and not good enough.
- I am going to overachieve and outshine everyone so that I can feel good enough.
- I am going to control the uncontrollable: people, circumstances, and events, so that I can feel good enough.

The problem is the sense of not being good enough has very strong connections in the neural net because it is often linked to intense feelings of disappointment from an early age; therefore, it is very difficult to simply compensate. Indeed, too often the counterbalancing mental models actually end up reinforcing the fundamental mental model. For example, if you fundamentally believe that you are not good enough, then being a perfectionist only makes it worse, since something is guaranteed to go wrong eventually. When you decide that you must control people, circumstances, and events and then end up feeling frustrated and inadequate when you cannot, it reinforces the mental model that you are not good enough. It is a difficult, self-perpetuating cycle in which many of us are caught. And yet it is *all in our minds*, a setup, our minds bringing us what we fundamentally believe! The key is to recognize and transform this common yet often paralyzing mental model. You can change your mind about yourself and everything else you experience in your world. You are the Subject!

Now that we have learned how often we misinterpret, misunderstand, and misjudge, is it possible that many of us have made a mistake about how to value ourselves? We already know that this common mental model of "not being good enough" does not serve us well. Is it possible that we are wrong? Is it possible that many of us have a common misperception about our value and worth? Could it be that every one of us is, in fact, good enough? What a thought! What would life be like for you if you framed your world around the knowledge and understanding that you are indeed good enough? Let's go back and remember our definition of objectivity. Objectivity is recognizing and accepting "what is," without projecting our fears, mental models, background, and experiences onto "what is." Therefore increasing your objectivity requires that you rethink and reframe the way you think about yourself.

Now that you have an overview of some common mental models to spark your thinking, the next step is to identify your own unique mental models, evaluate them, and transform those that no longer serve you.

IDENTIFYING YOUR OWN MENTAL MODELS

To identify the mental models that impede your ability to see things as they are and respond objectively requires a process of self-reflection. The process that has proven most helpful in my classes and workshop are the exercises in this book. In Exercise 1 in Chapter 2, I asked you to reflect on a situation in which you responded less than objectively. Asking yourself why you felt a certain way and what the underlying assumptions were can help identify a limiting mental model. For example, if you are constantly judging others at work and are beginning to get blowback as a result, you may have a Control mental model operating. If you are reading negative tone in e-mails and assuming that someone is always criticizing you, you may have a Perfectionist mental model, or the Insecurity: "I am not good enough" mental model may be dominating your responses. For example, do you frequently assume people are not taking you seriously, or that people are undermining you?

Your worldview is largely based on what you fundamentally think and feel about yourself. And as we have seen, your self-concept, in turn, is often formed by what people think of you and what you *think* others think of you. Therefore, the second reflection in Exercise 2 in Chapter 3 asked you to write what you think about yourself and what you think others think about you, and then reflect on whether you agree with the opinions of others. This often leads people to identify their overarching mental models, those that drive their approach to life generally.

The third reflection is to focus on your thoughts, also a part of Exercise 2 in Chapter 3. Since you are the Subject and are aware of your thoughts, jot down some of your recurring thoughts over a period of at least one week. What are you consistently thinking about or coming back to? What is the tone of those thoughts? Are they positive and accepting or negative and judgmental about yourself, other people, or both?

In addition, since you are aware of your fears, the fourth reflection is to help you uncover your fears by completing the last part of Exercise 2 in

Chapter 3. Write down what you are afraid of. As we have seen, fear is sometimes associated with something or someone external to you, and a negative assumption that you are making about that something or someone. Fear also comes up when there is or may be a disconnect between what you wanted or expected and reality. Think about what you are afraid of, and then think about the underlying assumption that makes you fear it. In addition, write down what you currently want and expect to happen in your life right now, and then jot down for each what you think will happen if what you want or expect doesn't happen. These exercises are reprinted here for your review.

ACTION PLAN: EXERCISE 1

STEP 1. ASSESSING YOUR CURRENT LEVEL OF OBJECTIVITY AND PINPOINTING YOUR HOT SPOTS (WHEN YOU ARE MORE SUBJECTIVE).

To start the process of increasing objectivity, begin by assessing how often you might respond less than objectively:

- How many times a day, week, or month do you overreact to situations?
- How many times a day, week, or month do you take things personally?

Once you have a sense of how often you are making cognitive errors, the next step is to pinpoint your hot spots by identifying what types of situations or interactions you are least objective about. Describe a professional situation where you were less than objective. Jot down your answers to the following questions:

- What is the objective reality of what happened?
- What was the cognitive error? What did you think was happening?
- What was your response?

- Looking back, what could have been a more appropriate response?
- What did it cost you?

Please repeat this exercise for a personal situation.

ACTION PLAN: EXERCISE 2

WHAT DO YOU FUNDAMENTALLY BELIEVE ABOUT YOURSELF?

How you frame your world is directly related to what you think about yourself. Often, our self-concept or what we think about ourselves is a combination of what we think and what we think others think. Therefore, jot down:

- What you think about yourself, for example, *I am smart, I am hardworking, I am friendly…*
- Write down what you think others think of you.
- Notice the difference between what you think and what they think. Why do you think there is a difference?

Your thoughts shape who you are and how you feel and often support underlying mental models. Think about and be aware of your thoughts. Jot down:

- The content of your stream of thoughts.
- Are your thoughts supportive, or neutral, or unsupportive?
- If some of your thoughts are judgmental or harsh, what do you say to yourself?
- What could be an underlying mental model or belief for that thought?
- Is it true?

FEAR.

- What you are afraid of?
- What are the mental models or underlying assumptions that make you fear it?
- What do you want or expect to happen?
- What do you think will happen if what you want or expect doesn't happen?

Reflect on these four data points: (1) a situation where you were less than objective; (2) what you think about yourself and what others think, and the intersection between the two, if any; (3) the general content of your thoughts; and (4) what you fear and the reason why you fear it. These are very useful tools to help you identify mental models that may be getting in your way.

Once you have reflected on these four data points, it is also useful to go back to the common mental models described in this chapter: External Validation, Competition, Perfectionist, Control, and Insecurity: "I am not good enough." Do any of these models, or a combination of these models, sound like you? In what way? Based on the four data points and the common examples, try to articulate clearly the mental model that you feel is no longer serving you. Take out a piece of paper and write down the answer to this question: What is it that you fundamentally believe is true about yourself and the world? Here are a few very specific mental models clearly articulated by workshop and class participants:

- If and when I have children, a rain cloud will follow me around professionally, and others will perceive me as less dedicated and committed to my profession.
- I have to be an expert at everything I do. Having all the answers implies that you are capable and intelligent.

- The man in a relationship should be the dominant one.
- Time and opportunities are limited, so I have to push for what I want now or it will never happen.
- Whenever possible, take emotions out of the equation. Emotions cloud rational thought and sound judgment. It is a sign of weakness. Just as one can control the body, one should control one's emotional responses.

Once you have clearly articulated your mental models, it is important to think back to when you might have formed that model or models. In classes and workshops, I provide executive coaching to help participants identify a primary underlying mental model that they may want to tweak or transform. Using the four data points, we are often able to uncover a situation in the past, sometimes all the way back to when they were kids, that led them to arrive at the conclusion that ultimately framed their world. Often this childhood experience was emotionally intense for the person, which created a strong mental model that was then reinforced in the person's memory. It is important that you reflect back on this situation so that you can understand and accept the underlying assumptions you made at the time. Often, the assumptions that you made as a child made sense, whether the assumptions were actually true or not. It is important for you to know that you were completely innocent, that you could not have drawn a different conclusion based on the circumstances. If you have a child around the same age, ask yourself, What would my child think under the same circumstances? Could the circumstances have been my child's fault? Could my child have arrived at a different conclusion? Once you are able to see that the mental model you formed was understandable under the circumstances, the next step is for you to make the determination that it no longer serves you to frame your world through that same lens. It is with this recognition and self-acceptance that true transformation can take place.

TRANSFORMING YOUR MENTAL MODELS

Once you have identified which mental model no longer serves you and you are able to articulate it clearly, the next step is to transform your old mental model. It is important to discount, refute, deem ineffective the current model and develop a new thought system or mental model that serves you better.

One of the most powerful transformational catalysts is *knowledge*, new information or logic that defies old mental models and ways of thinking. As we have seen, mental models are deep-rooted beliefs, ideas, and notions that we tend to hold onto, no matter what. They've usually been with us a while, so we tend to trust them, in some cases justifiably. I cannot tell you that your Perfectionist mental model does not serve you well. You have to decide, through your own logic and reason, whether your way of seeing the world is no longer valid for you. This requires that you be open to new knowledge, information, and reasoning. It is in the wake of this new knowledge that transformation takes place. Mark Jung-Beeman of Northwestern University's Institute for Neuroscience and others call it a "moment of insight" and have used MRI and EEG technologies to study how they happen. The findings suggest that at a moment of insight, an adrenaline-like chemical is released and a complex set of new connections are created in the brain.[5] It's these new connections that have the potential to enhance our mental resources to help us transform limiting mental models.

To help facilitate a moment of insight, I use the following Principles of Objectivity. These are truths that we all intuitively understand and can be verified through our own personal experience, yet we tend to take them for granted or discount them altogether. These Principles of Objectivity created moments of insight for me and were extremely helpful in transforming the mental models that undoubtedly contributed to my loss of a million dollars.

PRINCIPLE 1: THERE WILL ALWAYS BE SITUATIONS THAT WE DON'T LIKE.

We all know that what can go wrong, will go wrong. But often when things happen that we don't expect or anticipate, we start the mini-movie titled *Why me, this always happens to me.* We start playing back memories of all the things that have gone wrong lately. Some of us react by disowning the problem or, worse yet, engaging in wishful thinking, willing the problem to go away on its own. Of course, in most cases, it won't.

In order to effectively handle day-to-day problems, the first step is to accept that they exist. Acceptance of "what is" is a precondition to right action. Nonacceptance is an ideal condition for an emotional, subjective reaction, and we have already learned how that can end. Furthermore, nonacceptance does not alter the fact that there is a problem. It just creates a chain of further emotional reactions that make the problem worse. If you are objective in your perception of a situation, you can then respond to it appropriately. The key is to accept a problem as it occurs and not take it personally.

This principle provided the following moment of insights to students.

A career woman in her mid-30s, Mary works for an investment bank and is very focused on her career. She shares:

> By keeping this principle in the forefront of my mind, along with a deep
> breath in and out, I will be more flexible in the moment. I like having
> a plan, and I currently get irritated when deviations from the plan arise.
> Rather than spending valuable time complaining and irritating those
> around me, if I can recall this principle, I can more easily adapt to what
> is now in front of me. In addition to being more adaptable, it will allow
> me to be more easygoing, both in work and in my personal life.

Phillip, 40 years old with a successful career in IT, responds to the principle this way:

> This is another way of saying that every situation is different, and
> things will not always go according to plan. This principle is the

most frustrating for me, and I find that it is the one that my mental models most often have difficulty framing. I would not call myself a perfectionist, but I do take a lot of pride in what I do, so I want everything to work—all the time. I always enter a new endeavor with a plan and an idea of how I will make the situation work to my advantage, so when it doesn't work out, I can become very frustrated. I feel helpless and find myself wanting to lash out as I see things going off course. In my head, I know that not every situation will go according to plan or that some situations are simply no-win situations, but it doesn't stop me from getting angry or upset when things don't go my way. In general, I think that if I were able to accept this idea that I may not be successful in every situation, I would probably be a lot happier and relaxed, but this one is really hard for me.

Josh, a 30-year-old serial entrepreneur, describes it like this:

The principle definitely changed my mental model of myself and the world around me. It made me happier in life to realize that being content with what happens to me is a matter of how I choose to perceive it. No one is out there to "get me" and no one is responsible for my state of mind. Only I can change my state of mind, and how I react to events. I look at events at their face value, just as events that happen. Some are good and some are bad, but how I turn a bad thing around is up to me.

PRINCIPLE 2: PEOPLE ARE FUNDAMENTALLY THE SAME, BUT EACH IS UNIQUE.

There is always a spirited debate about this principle, so it is important to understand the context. The Human Genome Project has confirmed that we are all fundamentally the same! Of the three billion DNA base pairs, only 0.1 percent distinguishes each of us from anyone else on the planet. In addition to our genetic similarity, we are all fundamentally the same in terms of our basic needs and desires. Everyone wants to be healthy, successful, have a good job, earn a good living, be loved, take care of their family, et cetera. Some may say these universal desires are also a part of our DNA. In the context of objectivity, this means that we can assume that everyone has formed mental models through which they frame their world based on their unique experiences. We can assume that just like you, everyone has a unique frame of reference; just like you, everyone else is thinking and acting through mental models they are probably not aware of. For example, many people have the common mental model that they are not good enough and are trying to minimize that feeling by aspiring to be perfect. Many of us are looking for someone to validate us, tell us that we are okay. Many people are worried about their health or their children or their careers. When you really think about it, in these ways we are all fundamentally the same.

A difficult challenge for many of us is the desire to control other people. Many of us get frustrated when someone doesn't act the way we want them to. We want them to be like us and see the world the way we do, and respond to us in the same way that we would respond to them. We often get angry when we are unable to change people. But the true source of this anger is often our lack of acceptance that people are fundamentally the same. That is, other people behave as they do because of their unique frames of reference, because of what is hardwired in their neural nets—just like you respond the way you do because of what is wired in your neural net.

Being objective means understanding and accepting that people are fundamentally the same and allowing them to be who they are. If you expect people to conform to your desires, then it is your own unfulfilled expectation that causes you anger. Instead of trying to change the other person and getting angry at them when they don't change, objectivity demands that you understand and accept another person's point of view or frame of reference. By accepting this principle and allowing people to be who they are, you will create more collaborative relationships at work and happier, more sustainable relationships at home.

Patricia, a 30-year-old career woman and mother, describes her moment of insight as:

> Understanding and accepting this principle will have a large impact on my career. While I try to put myself in other's shoes during consulting engagements and change initiatives, I can think of times when I have totally forgotten that my boss also has mental models and might be acting a certain way because of an emotion that has nothing to do with me. For example, what I might perceive as a lack of risk taking and leadership, as well as micromanaging, might be caused by many mental models. Realizing that other people have similar patterns and can get on a "crazy train" of thought sometimes will make me more aware of the facts, the "what is," rather than projecting mental models onto something and boarding the crazy train myself.

Lawrence, a corporate attorney in his late 40s with a family, struggles with this a bit and says,

> If we conclude that people are fundamentally the same, I think that goes against what I've been told for most of my life, which is that everyone is different and that is okay (usually). I suppose that when it gets down to the hierarchy of needs, then fundamentally, yes we are all the same. Everyone needs to be safe and secure, have a sense of family or community, food, water, et cetera. Thinking about it now, I suppose that I often do not think that fundamentally everyone is the same. At work, if someone did not do something that was supposed to be done or perhaps not the way that I would have done it, there is a small piece of me that always thinks, why did that person do it that way when they should have done it this way? I tend to be a tough judge of character, and if I don't see someone working "hard" by my definition, then I can't help but be a little critical. But at the end of the day, almost everyone is working for their families, to put

food on the table or take care of their children or trying to provide a better life for themselves. When I go to work tomorrow, I am going to try and remember that people are fundamentally the same. I think it will allow me to relate to people better, and in doing so, will enable me to become a much stronger leader. If people are able to relate to one another, then it creates a strong, effective, successful team. By looking at people through the lens of "people are fundamentally the same," I think it will allow me to potentially change some of the mental models that I have of others, and perhaps be a little less critical of them.

LESSON LEARNED

I learned that objectivity includes accepting that people may see the world differently than I do. I assumed that my supplier would see things as I did. My way of thinking was that our company is responsible for navigating US Customs and the FDA labeling process for the supplier to gain access to the US market. We were 75 percent of US sales thus far, poised with commitments from new distribution channels. The supplier would never hurt their number one distributor. That made no sense!

Well, it did make sense for the supplier. Perhaps a business in the United States would never hurt their top distributor, but this assumption is based on how we do business here, not considering what could be at play in South Africa. Being objective means realizing that everyone has their own frame of reference and point of view. The most important thing you can do in any relationship, personal or professional, is to understand another person's frame of reference. Being objective means asking questions to seek clarity about the motivations, assumptions, conclusions, and beliefs of the other person.

PRINCIPLE 3: WE CANNOT ALWAYS CONTROL THE RESULTS OF OUR ACTIONS.

Have you ever worked on a project and done your absolute best, but the project still failed? Almost everyone has. Many of us believe that there are only two possible results to every effort, success or failure. What dictates the results, and the varying degrees of success or failure? The reality is that we cannot control hidden variables, the things that are unknown and the things that are unknowable. The only way to be ready for these hidden variables is by doing what needs to be done and by being objective to the results. The highly revered Vendanta scholar Swami Dayananda Saraswati calls this the *yoga of objectivity*, which is also well known as karma-yoga from the Bhagavad Gita.[6] The challenge for many of us is that we have been socialized to (1) value ourselves based on the end result rather than the process or the effort, and (2) to value others based on results rather than the process or effort.

Being objective means understanding and accepting the fact that you have limited control over hidden variables. But we have absolute control over our choice of action and performing the action itself. We can only do our absolute best in the present moment, and all our anxiety about the way things will turn out won't change the result. But instead of thinking about the task at hand, our minds tend to project into the future with thoughts such as, *If I fail, I won't be able to buy that new house or send my children to college.* To achieve greater results requires staying focused in the present moment and putting all of our attention on the action we choose, and then performing that action.

Cynthia, a married mother of three in her mid-30s who is a director of a call center, had the following moment of insight in response to this principle:

> I certainly think I can control the results of my actions. I have many pre-conceived notions about what the result should be when I act a certain

way. This mostly plays out for me in how I think others should respond to me based on my actions. If I am nothing but nice and generous with someone, then they should recognize it. If I help someone out, I should be promoted. These expectations on my part have often led me to feel disappointment and hurt when what I expected didn't happen. That disappointment and hurt causes me to act differently the next time the situation occurs. The only thing I can do is control my own actions. I will never be able to control how other people react to me or what result my action might bring. Accepting this reality is going to help me not feel hurt or disappointed when the results I expected don't happen. There are always factors contributing to that result that I can do nothing about. I can't take it personally when someone forgets to thank me for something I did, or when I don't get that promotion that I felt I should. The other person could have been distracted and merely forgot to thank me. Maybe I wasn't promoted because the company is actually downsizing, or there is some other opportunity that I should be looking into. All I can do is make sure that I am doing the best that I can, and the results will be what they are. Accepting this principle, not just the previous three principles, will allow me to be nicer to myself. By taking personally things that are really outside my control, I'm only hurting myself. I am starting to realize that I need to ban the word "should" from my vocabulary and thinking. *There are no shoulds, there is only "what is."* To be objective is to accept "what is," and then move on.

Francis, a teacher at a local high school who is married with one son, said,

Our actions matter. Unless we make good choices, we are more likely to have bad outcomes to situations. The fact is that we do not control what results come from our choices and actions. We would be wise to accept a power greater than ourselves so that we do not stress ourselves over the uncontrollable outcomes of our actions. All we can do is make the best choices possible, and hope for the best.

Forgetting this principle, that I cannot control the world around me, no matter how good my choices and actions are, has caused me some considerable stress over the years. In the past, when I made a choice and took action, I stressed over whether I would achieve the result I wanted so much that I began to suffer from anxiety. I drove myself crazy, rethinking everything, wondering whether I did things right and what would happen to me if it didn't turn out the way I wanted. For years, this mental model was very damaging because when things did not go my way, I felt that I had failed personally and now I know that that is not true. Lately, I have focused only upon what I can do, my choices in any given moment. This means that I have been experiencing less stress over what should happen, and have been able to take more joy in outcomes that are less than what I originally desired or expected. The fact is that I can control very little other than my actions.

PRINCIPLE 4: EVERYTHING IS CONNECTED, INTERRELATED.

As we saw earlier, increasing our objectivity includes rethinking and reframing the way we think about ourselves. After experiencing a significant failure in business, learning how to value and accept myself again was a game changer for me. I was able to develop a line of reasoning, a new way to frame my world, a new mental model that I was indeed good enough. This new mental model became the foundation for a new self-concept that is less dependent on external validation. This principle sparked the greatest moment of insight for me, which enabled me to finally get off the couch. Here is my line of reasoning that changed everything:

As human beings, it is clear that we did not choose the world we find ourselves in, nor do we have control over much of it. The earth revolves, the sun generates energy, changes in ocean temperature in one part of the world affect weather patterns in other parts of the world, and so on. It all works together, everything having a purpose and connected to everything else. It is also apparent that living beings are interconnected and interrelated and each is born with its own inherent capacity to grow, develop, and reach its fullest potential. For example, each caterpillar has within itself the inherent capacity and everything it needs to morph into a beautiful butterfly. Within every acorn seed, as another example, is the inherent potential to become an oak tree. Within each acorn seed is the potential root structure, the branch structure, the leaf structure and function, the process for chlorophyll loss that controls the change of colors, and everything else required to become an oak tree. These are just two obvious examples in our natural world of this inherent capacity. The key for me was to realize that this same interconnectedness and inherent capacity applied to me—and to all other people. Think about it. You did not choose your gender, your race, your parents or their socioeconomic status, your siblings, or where you were born. You also didn't choose what you love or what you are good at. At some point you *realized* that you loved chocolate, hated lima beans, and were good at sports. But you didn't choose it, it just is the way it is. Just like the sun, the moon, gravity, the weak force, the strong force, electromagnetic force, and all other aspects of our world, it just is. When I dug a little deeper to try to validate for myself the notion that everything that just is, is in fact interconnected and interrelated, I thought about one of my science lessons in grade school—photosynthesis. Photosynthesis is a process used by plants and other organisms to convert light energy, normally from the Sun, into chemical energy that can be later released to fuel the organisms' activities. This chemical energy is stored in carbohydrate molecules, such as sugars, which are synthesized from carbon dioxide and water. In most cases, oxygen is also released as a waste product. It is the process of photosynthesis that maintains atmospheric oxygen levels and supplies all of the organic compounds and most of the energy necessary for life on Earth.[7] Wow; not only do most plants, algae, and certain types of bacteria perform photosynthesis to support their own survival, their function and purpose is also key to everyone and everything else's survival. Although this is just one example, this was the clincher for me. So I put it all together in my mind. Just like everything else in our natural world, each of us is born with unique abilities and the potential to fully express them, and we have a purpose and function that is connected to everything else. This was an "aha" moment for me. I thought to myself, *How could I not be good enough as I am if, with my unique combination of gifts and skills, I have a purpose and a function that is connected to everyone and everything else?* This definitely got me off the couch. I was beginning to see myself differently. But frankly, deep down I still wished I hadn't lost a million dollars. After all, none of my friends lost a million dollars and had to start over. Although I knew that I had core gifts and skills, I was still struggling with "why me." I was off the couch but I still desperately needed to know what happened, what went wrong, and what I could have done better. I was still beating myself up, and admittedly there were times when my thoughts would devolve into blaming and accusing others. After a while, I realized that I was just hurting myself with this line of thinking and none of that mattered. Another moment of insight came when I began to realize that even our circumstances, successes and failures, pains and losses (which, by the way, we also did not choose), continue to shape us, helping us grow into our fullest potential, and are connected to everything else. I resolved that it wasn't about why it happened; it was all about how the experience could help me grow. And that *was* my choice.

Many people have shared stories of difficult childhood experiences that they look back on with anger and disappointment. It is important to understand that just as we didn't choose our race, gender, eye color, or hair color, in most cases we didn't choose nor could we control our circumstances. No one chooses to have a mentally ill parent. No one chooses to have a sister with Down syndrome. No one chooses to witness a horrible accident that causes a friend's death. These things are also a part of "what is," and they too shape who we are. Your circumstances become part of who you are. It is important to think not just about the negative consequences of these circumstances and the limiting mental models that you may have developed as a result, but also about all the skills and unique perspectives you may have gained from those experiences. For example, Sharon, a brilliant and kind woman in her early 30s whose mother was mentally ill, had to learn self-sufficiency and independence at an early age, which served her well in her entrepreneurial venture. Ralph, a very successful engineer in his early 40s whose family was dysfunctional, was forced to assume great responsibility at a young age and became very resourceful, trustworthy, and dependable. Regardless of the circumstances that you had to manage, accepting them as a part of "what is"—and as something to leverage as part of your unique experience, gifts, and potential—is the key to objectivity.

The next moment of insight for me was clearly seeing that it was illogical to compare myself with others. When trying to stay off the couch, it was not helpful for me to compare myself to others and replay mini-movies in my mind about how it wasn't fair that I had to start over and others didn't. Since I fully accepted the new mental model that I was indeed good enough, I had to rethink how I thought about myself relative to others. No one else has the same setup as I do, not even my twin sister (she likes milk chocolate and peanut butter, and I like dark chocolate and hate peanut butter). The truth is that we all are unique, in our abilities, in our circumstances, and in our purposes. It became clear to me that our power comes from fully leveraging all that we are. It does not come from projecting a false image that we think others want and expect. Instead of comparing ourselves with others and feeling inadequate, we must value and accept ourselves based on our unique combination of core strengths, gifts, and experiences. Everything we are is unique to us, from our DNA to where we were born and to whom we were born, which uniquely shapes who we are. I thought to myself: *How can I think I am less than or not good enough in comparison with another woman when I grew up with a twin sister, two half-brothers, and*

two working parents, while the other woman grew up in California, with
no siblings and a stay-at-home mom?

This helped me not only stay off the couch but gave me the confidence
to get back out there. I could now see that my unique gifts, skills, and
even my sometimes annoying idiosyncrasies combined with my circumstances and made me who I am. Objectivity is about seeing and accepting
"what is." You are a part of what is, so that includes you.

I actually got to the point where I truly accepted and appreciated
everything about myself, including losing a million dollars. Can you
imagine? Although gut-wrenching and excruciating at the time, if I hadn't
lost a million dollars, I know now that I wouldn't be the happiest I have
ever been, teaching at Babson College and writing about objectivity. For
me this principle changed everything. I see myself now as a masterpiece
in the making. Now, the only thing I have to do every morning is get up
and be the best I can be in every moment, leveraging all that I am. And
yes, sometimes the results change. Sometimes I am tired, sometimes other
people are tired; I don't control any of that. My freedom and joy comes
from knowing that everything is interconnected and interrelated and that
my power in this world comes from being objective—seeing and accepting myself as I am, and fearlessly being who I am!

This fourth principle resonated for other people in the following
ways.

Cathy, a reporter at a local news station in her early 30s, had the following moment of insight:

> Accepting that I am part of the order of the universe and "what
> is" is difficult for me sometimes. There are things in my past,
> such as a tumultuous relationship with my parents and my bro-
> ken engagement, that lead me to my mental model of "I am not
> good enough," which is not healthy and prevents me from being
> objective. Sometimes I wish that I could change my past, but I am
> beginning to accept that who I am and where I am today is because

of everything that has happened in my life. I am much more at ease when I consciously accept this. For example, as an undergrad I transferred colleges and wound up at Smith. I absolutely loved it there, and I used to wish that I had spent all four years there rather than two and a half. However, some of the best friends I made at school I met in my transfer orientation group. It is unlikely that I ever would have become good friends with those individuals had we not had that orientation in common. More recently, I think about my current relationship. As painful as my last breakup was, I can easily say it was well worth it for the relationship I have now. Had my ex and I not broken up when we did, or had I not started dating again when I did, I never would have met my boyfriend.

Just writing about these connections makes me happy and helps me to accept who I am, as well as new situations that arise in my life. I begin to see that it is not that "I am not good enough," but rather that I am a work in progress and every situation that arises shapes me to be who I am. The way I choose to handle situations can create positive or negative outcomes. The more objective I can be, the more likely I will be satisfied with the outcome.

George, a very competitive stock broker in his late 30s, describes his moment of insight this way:

Understanding that I am a part of "what is" and that everything is interrelated will allow me to remember to accept how I am, where I have been, and focus on where I am going. From a personal and professional standpoint, I feel that remembering this principle will decrease my jealousy and envy of other people. There is nothing I could have done to change my upbringing or alter anyone else's, so I should not spend any energy trying to change it or wish it was different. Thinking about this principle will allow me to rethink my mental model of "I am not the best at anything" and will hopefully make me pause before I start comparing myself to everyone. I am an individual, an individual who is part of everything else, and I am doing my best with what I've got.

I have found that many people do not recognize their unique combination of skills, gifts, and talents. On the contrary, many people are so good at projecting a false image and acting the way that they think they should that they simply no longer know the truth about themselves, who they really are. This can be a very frightening feeling. Many people found it useful to engage in Exercise 5 at the end of this chapter to remember their unique gifts and talents and connect with who they are. This exercise is summarized below:

Jot down what you absolutely love. What makes you feel silly or joyful? Think about a moment when you weren't judging something or complaining about something, a moment when you just enjoyed what you were experiencing and were not trying to change it. When you are just experiencing something without judgment, in that moment you are happy and you are totally being yourself. The next step is to ask someone in your life who has known you since you were a child what kind of little kid you were. What did you like? What did you play with? Were you friendly and warm, or were you tense? Often, people find out a lot about who they are at their core by asking their primary caregiver. The final step is to write down what you absolutely love about yourself and what you believe is your core gift, not based on what anyone else says and not compared to anyone else. Generally, everyone is able to come up with a few things they feel good about.

Being objective requires a deep understanding of who and what you are. Taking stock, acknowledging your strengths and your limitations, and realizing that those strengths and the limitations are all a part of "what is" is the basis of objectivity. Many people embark on a path of self-development in order to fix something, with the underlying assumption that there is something wrong with them, thereby reinforcing a negative self-concept in the neural net. Being objective means accepting yourself as you are today—with the capacity and desire to grow and to reach your full potential. It is your inherent nature to do so. Remembering this subtle distinction will help greatly in creating and sustaining the growth and development you seek.

SUPPORTING YOUR NEW MENTAL MODEL

Using these principles to spark moments of insight for yourself is critical for transforming old mental models. To further support the transformation process, it is important to link these moments of insight with new experiences that categorically refute old ways of thinking and acting. Now this can get interesting. Your mind, on automatic pilot, will normally support preexisting mental models. If you think about an experience that refutes an old mental model, your mind may come up with anecdotal data to convince you that your experience does in fact support your old way of thinking and acting. But as we learn to take control of our appraisal process and consciously bring concepts and assumptions up to our prefrontal cortex for evaluation, we can retrain our brains to respond differently.

Specifically, when you are in the process of reflecting on your mental models in the context of the four principles of objectivity, it is helpful to think of experiences you've had that support your new line of reasoning. For example, if you are focusing on transforming your Control mental model, and you have a moment of insight regarding principle #3 (you cannot always control the results of your actions), then, in your reflection, try to think of—or better yet, write down—situations and experiences when the unknowable, the unpredictable, and uncontrollable did in fact influence the end result. More importantly, write down what you learned from those experiences and what you will do the next time you face similar situations.

CHANGING YOUR RESPONSE, REWIRING YOUR NEURAL NET

While the principles, moments of insight, and links to experiences helps you consciously discard the old mental model and accept the new one, the next step is to put it in action. Your goal now is for the new mental model to steer your behavior, not the unproductive and limiting one. The next step is to go back to the mental models that you identified that are no longer serving you, and write down what triggers, behaviors, or thoughts that mental model invokes. Then write down a new way of thinking and a new way of responding. Remember, the key to transforming mental models is to interrupt the automatic responses that are driven by the old model and respond differently based on the new model. Each time you are able to do this, you are actually loosening the old circuit and creating new neural connections in your brain. Being aware of how your old mental model gets triggered and the current behavior it invokes is the first step in the process of rewiring your neural net. Here are a few examples:

Old Mental Model	Current Behavior/ Triggers	New Mental Model	New Response
Everything in life has to be structured, with routines and habits that provide security.	I try to impose control on everything and everyone. I become inpatient and judgmental when people don't think the same way or do things the way I want. Triggers: I feel angry and frustrated, like I am going to explode.	I can't control all situations, especially the uncontrollable or unknowable. I have confidence that I can handle any situation that comes my way. People have valuable perspectives that I should consider if I want to be a good leader.	Stop, be in the moment without anticipating what will happen next in order to try to control it. Be more patient, seek out other's perspectives and recognize the merits of those other ideas.
I need external validation and recognition to feel happy.	Needing constant recognition makes me feel anxious, always looking for	I recognize, value, and am confident in my innate gifts and skills that I have used	I will ask myself if I am doing this for me or for recognition. If it is not for me

(Continued)

Old Mental Model	Current Behavior/ Triggers	New Mental Model	New Response
Getting recognition is the primary motivator for my life. I need to be the star!	the next thing to be recognized for. I often begrudge others for a job well done or a well-deserved promotion or opportunity. Triggers: My heart races when I feel this anxiety; I become warm.	successfully in my life, therefore I don't need someone else to recognize my value in order for me to feel happy.	alone, then I will not take it on. I will go out of my way to compliment and recognize someone else for their accomplishments.
I believe that I have to be the best at everything I do.	I put too much pressure on myself, creating stress and anxiety. I compare myself to others and feel jealous or resentful of others. Triggers: I feel a pit in my stomach and sometimes a little nausea.	I believe that I can only do my best every day with whatever the circumstances are, and I will accept whatever happens next.	I will not seek out information about how others did. I will only focus on my performance and whether I did my best.

Each time you respond differently, you are enabling new neurons to wire together. To help the new connections continue to fire together requires focus and attention. The term *attention density* refers to the attention paid to a particular mental experience over a specific time. The greater the concentration on a specific idea or mental experience, the higher the attention density. With enough attention density, new brain circuitry can be stabilized. Individual thoughts can become an intrinsic part of an individual's identity, permanently changing how he perceives the world and how his brain works. Neuroscientists call this "self-directed neuroplasticity."[8]

The challenge is that it does take time. And during the process, situations may arise that trigger an automatic response. While mindfulness will help you respond more objectively in the moment, it is helpful, after the fact, to reflect back on those situations through your new lens.

One self-reflection tool to help you increase the attention density for a newly wired mental model is cognitive restructuring, a technique used in cognitive-behavioral therapy to identify and correct negative thinking patterns. The technique includes altering negative automatic thoughts that occur in anxiety-provoking situations (such as *They think I'm boring*) by replacing them with more rational beliefs (such as *I can't read other people's minds; they are probably just tired*). As thoughts are challenged and disputed, their power to elicit anxiety is lessened. In cognitive restructuring, you consciously take charge of the appraisal process to ensure your conclusions are accurate and free of biases and mistakes. The following step-by-step process has proven to be valuable to my students and workshop participants:

1. Reflect on a situation or event—what happened? Write down verbatim some of the thoughts that were going through your head at the time. How were you feeling as a result of those thoughts? How did you respond?

2. What sorts of cognitive errors could be present in your thoughts? What mental models/biases are present in your thoughts? What are the underlying assumptions behind those thoughts and mental models?

3. What new mental models can replace the old one? Which moment of insight can help you rethink the old mental model that drove your response? What experience have you had that supports the new mental model? What new thoughts can support the new mental model?

4. How do you feel contemplating the new mental model? Stay with the positive feeling for several minutes. How will you respond next time, based on this new mental model?

Transforming mental models is a process. It takes time, energy, and focus. Some are easier to transform than others. Of the students surveyed,

69 percent reported that they were *somewhat successful* in shifting a mental model; 25 percent said they were *very successful*. All said that it requires motivation and attention. Sixty-three percent of students surveyed said they are consistently and consciously working on the shift, while 19 percent reported that they reflect weekly on the shift. Ideally, as you shift limiting and unproductive mental models, you will notice that you begin to see things as they are and respond more objectively, which is the best motivation to keep at it.

It is important that you start off slowly. Mental models drive our responses in various ways in different aspects of our lives. It is helpful to choose a mental model and work first on changing *one* way it may play out in your life—preferably the one least likely to disrupt your life. For example, Peter, a director of operations for a law firm with a very strong Control mental model, started with his drive to work. One of the ways his need to control played out for him was that he arrived to work angry and exhausted every day. He became visibly and audibly angry and impatient when driving to work, primarily because of the way people drove. He realized that is was just his need to control things; in reality, people were not getting up at five o'clock in the morning and leaving their houses at a precise time to conspire to drive slowly, change lanes without signaling, talk on their cell phones, or put on their lipstick just to slow him down. Yet these things made him very anxious. He began to remind himself that he could not control traffic patterns or how people drove. He reasoned that they were probably just as anxious about getting to work on time as he was. He decided to first try to shift this one Control mental model pattern. He began leaving his house earlier, taking a more scenic route to work, and paying more attention to how hard he was gripping the steering wheel. After a few weeks, he arrived at work calm, focused, and not spoiling for a fight.

It is absolutely critical while in the process of shifting a mental model to be kind to yourself. Remember that your old ways of responding have been hardwired, and it takes time, patience, and focus to shift it. Every time you are impatient with yourself, and disappointed in your response, you end up strengthening the old connection that you are not good enough, the connection you are trying to rewire. You can't be mad at your mind. Instead, have fun with it. When you find yourself doing what you normally do, just smile; acknowledge that it is the nature of the mind and that you will make the changes you desire in time. You are the Subject. Again, you have the power to change your mind. Exercise 5 will help you identify your unique combination of talents and abilities so that you can learn to be more objective about yourself.

ACTION PLAN: EXERCISE 5

Uncover your unique gifts and skills so that you can learn to value them:

- Jot down what you absolutely love.
- What makes you feel silly or joyful?

Ask someone in your life who has known you since you were a child:

- What kind of little kid you were.
- What did you like?
- What did you play with?
- Were you friendly and warm, or were you serious, tense?

Write down what you absolutely love about yourself and what you believe are your core gifts, not based on what anyone else says and not compared to anyone else.

Part IV

THE OBJECTIVE LEADER

Chapter 7

CREATING INCLUSIVE ENVIRONMENTS

So far we have seen how often we tend to overreact to situations and take things personally. Unfortunately, our lack of objectivity also spills over into how we judge and respond to people. As we have seen, leaders hire, motivate, manage, and develop others. Leaders are often measured by the results they achieve, which is often dependent on how well they motivate, manage, and develop. Invariably, in corporate performance appraisals, management and leadership skills are central evaluation criteria. The challenge is that we often misjudge people—sometimes based on what they look like, what they're wearing, or perhaps what they sound like. In fact, in our objectivity survey, we found that 75 percent of people responded that they misjudged someone at least once a month or more; the survey also found that 23.4 percent said they misjudged someone based on their appearance 2 or 3 times per month; 9.4 percent said once a month; 17.4 percent said 2 or 3 times per week; and 4.7 percent said they misjudged someone, simply based on their appearance, *every day*.

Misjudgments not only impact our ability to manage and lead effectively; it can also be very costly for leaders of global companies seeking to maintain or establish a business relationship in emerging markets where people, cultures, and customs are different. And of course, it can undermine the efforts of leaders of domestically focused companies seeking to diversify their workforce for competitive advantage in an increasingly diverse US demographic. The question is, how often are you misjudging people, and what is it costing you?

As Babson College's first chief diversity officer from 2008 to 2011, I often conduct corporate objectivity seminars to help senior leaders fully leverage the business case for diversity and inclusion. Recently, I facilitated a two-day meeting with the Global Diversity and Inclusion Council of a global company with 38,000 employees operating in 70 countries. During the offsite meeting, one of the corporate presidents said, "As global leaders, we all understand the business case for diversity and inclusion. It is imperative that we learn how to effectively lead diverse teams and develop multicultural approaches to problem solving and decision making. The problem is that many of my people think that diversity and inclusion is like a tax; we have to pay it but no one likes to talk about it."

I asked the group, "If we framed the conversation in the context of objectivity as a core competency for effective leadership, would your people perceive this as a tax?" They all responded no. We spent the rest of the two days reframing the global diversity and inclusion initiative as an opportunity for leaders across the organization to become more objective about the way they respond to daily challenges, including people that are different from them. In fact, we not only reframed the conversation, we renamed the initiative: Global Inclusion and Objectivity.

The global inclusion and objectivity conversation must begin with the acknowledgement that we are all biased, whether we are male or female; Christian, Muslim, or agnostic; African American, Asian American, or Caucasian; from China, Malaysia, India, or Iran; heterosexual, homosexual, or transgender; able bodied or disabled. It is the nature of the mind. When we talk about culture or any other way in which we are different from each other, the mind is functioning in precisely the same subjective way it responds to everything else, and we have already learned that we can't be mad at our minds.

When we see a person who is different from us, our mind instantly perceives the difference. There is no problem here; no shame, no blame. The problem is what happens next: we project our own mental models onto that perception of difference. That projection then forms the basis for our subjective and often prejudicial or stereotypical judgment of that person (good/bad, like/dislike, fear/trust), which then drives our behavior toward that person. What is so insidious is that we rarely question the mental models that form the basis for our subjective responses to the people we meet. But just as we can increase our objectivity regarding situations and events, we can also increase our objectivity regarding people.

As we have learned, objectivity is the ability to perceive and accept "what is" without projecting our mental models, including stereotypes and prejudices, onto the object being perceived. In this case, "what is" is a person who is different than us. Objectivity helps us accept that person and respond to them thoughtfully, deliberately, and effectively. In order to increase our objectivity regarding race, gender, sexual orientation, age, et cetera, we must understand how implicit biases are formed and how they act as drivers of subjectivity that trap us into old ways of thinking and responding.

WE ALL HAVE BIAS

Studies reveal that most of us have definite, entrenched stereotypes about blacks, women, the elderly, and other social groups by the age of five. For example, there have been recent studies that have recreated the infamous 1940s Clark Doll test that reveal children's attitudes about race. This Clark Doll experiment involved a child being presented with two dolls. Both of these dolls were completely identical except for the skin and hair color. One doll was white with yellow hair while the other was brown with black hair. The child was then asked questions about which doll they would play with, which one is the nice doll, which one looks bad, which one has the nicer color, et cetera. The experiment showed a clear preference for the white doll among all children in the study. This result was confirmed in a similar test conducted by CNN in 2010. In this test, white children, as a whole, responded with a high rate of what researchers call "white bias," identifying the color of their own skin with positive attributes and darker skin with negative attributes. In addition, even black children, as a whole, have some bias toward whiteness, but far less than white children. The CNN study concluded that children's ideas about race change little from age five to age ten.[1] Why does this happen?

As children, we experienced and interpreted our environment and formed conclusions about our world. If we didn't see black faces in our Saturday morning cartoons, we might have assumed that black was not as good. If we didn't see women holding positions of power, we may have concluded that women were not as smart as men. If we went to school and saw few, if any, black children, we might have made the assumptions that something was wrong with black people. We were just trying to make sense of our world. And no matter how progressive our parents were, as soon as we walked out the door, we had to confront peer pressure, the media, and the social structure that promulgated these stereotypes. As a result, many of us have unconscious biases that we are simply not aware of, hardwired into the brain's neural net. Again, there is no shame in this.

An ongoing study of implicit bias called the Implicit Association Test (IAT), developed by Harvard University professor Mahzarin Banaji and University of Washington professor Anthony Greenwald, resoundingly confirms this unsettling truth: "We all use stereotypes all the time, without knowing it. Although many of us think we're not prejudiced toward any group of people, our brain activity tells a different story."[2]

The IAT measures unconscious attitudes regarding skin color, age, sexuality, disability, and much more. The computer-based test requires users to rapidly categorize two concepts with an attribute by pressing the appropriate left-hand key (e) or right-hand key (i) (for example, the concepts "male" and "female" with the attribute "nurturing"). Easier pairings (faster responses) are interpreted as more strongly associated in memory than more difficult pairings (slower responses). Although still debated, data reported from the first 4.5 million tests revealed the following:

- People are often unaware of their implicit biases. Ordinary people, including the researchers who direct this project, harbor negative associations in relation to various social groups (i.e., implicit biases), even while honestly (the researchers believe) reporting that they regard themselves as lacking these biases.
- Implicit biases predict behavior. From simple acts of friendliness and inclusion to more consequential acts, such as the evaluation of work quality, those who are higher in implicit bias have been shown to display greater discrimination.
- People differ in levels of implicit bias. Implicit biases vary from person to person and can be a function of the person's group memberships, the dominance of a person's membership group in society, a person's consciously held attitudes, and the level of bias existing in the immediate environment.[3]

This last observation makes clear that implicit attitudes are modified by experience.

NO SHAME, NO BLAME

It is 2014, and still many of our conversations about race, gender, and all other forms of separatism are still centered on shame and blame. The corporate president from the global company is right: no one wants to talk about it if the conversation devolves into rehashing the women's movement, the civil rights movement, or the current inequities of gays and lesbians, et cetera. If you add religion to the mix, it gets even more uncomfortable. The challenge is that many people who are aware of their biases are ashamed of them. When we feel ashamed that we have bias, our tendency is to deny it, become defensive about it, and distance ourselves from it. To be effective leaders, we must learn to accept the fact that it is in our nature to have bias, and not just about race. It can be toward anyone who is different from us in any way. We must stop blaming each other and feeling ashamed of ourselves. We must also, however, hold ourselves accountable for our behavior toward one another and consciously choose to respond more inclusively.

It is essential, if we hope to be effective leaders in a diverse world, to understand our own biases. In many of my corporate training programs, I use the IAT to help corporate leaders become aware that they may have biases and to lead them through a process of transforming those biases. As we have seen, acknowledging our mental models is the first step in transforming them. Interestingly, this is a difficult experience for people. Even when they know, intellectually, that there is no shame in having biases they may have formed when they were four or five years old, many participants who receive a result suggesting that they might have a bias against African Americans, overweight people, or the elderly, for example, feel embarrassed. Understandably, most people do not like to think of themselves as being biased. We would prefer to think that we are fair, open-minded, and objective. The following examples represent common experiences with the IAT test results among executives.

- A white man was relieved and proud to learn that the IAT indicated that he had no preference for white over black. He was beaming. I asked him where he grew up. He said his father worked for the State Department, and he grew up with children from all over the world. The key point in his experience is that when he was forming associations to make sense of his environment, he confronted a world where there were children of different races, ethnicities, and religious backgrounds. His four- or five-year-old mind did not make any judgments or associations based on these attributes because it was normal to see a broad range of variations.

- A white woman admitted to feeling shame when her tests results revealed a slight preference for whites over blacks. She said she made a conscious effort to expose her kids to a diverse group of children because she wants them to learn the value of differences. In spite of her values and her efforts to be unbiased in her actions, it was possible that she still had an unconscious bias. She said she grew up in an all-white neighborhood and went to a predominately white school. The key point in her experience is that the associations she made were the result of her environment and that as a child she couldn't have drawn a different conclusion. It was important to reassure her and others like her that they should not feel shame for being biased, but they must continue to be vigilant so their biases don't steer discriminatory behavior. In her case it certainly never did.

- An African American man bravely admitted that his IAT results showed that he had a preference for white over black. He was shocked and embarrassed. He shared that he consciously exposed his children to positive models of African Americans, for instance, by buying both black and white Barbie dolls for his daughters. He added that when he was growing up he was constantly exposed to negative images of black people, both in his own environment and in what he often saw reported by the media. His result demonstrates the power of the media in the development and reinforcement of unconscious prejudices. It was important to reassure him that I have seen many responses similar to his, in which a person is biased against the group to which he or she belongs: women who sometimes feel conflicted at work because they associate women with family and men with careers; elderly people who see themselves and other elderly as less valuable because they have an automatic preference for young over old; and people who are overweight having a preference for thin people—often based on societal mental models.

The latter two examples above are the most instructive in helping you understand how you can change and become inclusive leaders of your organizations. Your conscious brain can lead you away from the prejudices of your hidden brain, your unconscious mind. Clearly the white woman's conscious values and choices led her away from any unconscious biases she developed growing up in a predominately white environment. Similarly, the African American man, in spite of influences that he may have encountered as a child that led him to become biased against his own group, made a conscious decision to think and act differently.

Banaji and Greenwald say, "To the extent that we can influence what we learn and believe, we can influence less conscious states of mind. We can determine who we are and who we wish to be."[4] This is very powerful! As we have learned, you are the Subject and everything you experience is an object to you and is not you. You can determine your response to everything you experience, including people who are not like you. Unfortunately, we have to admit that while many of us are ashamed of our biases and try to overcome them, some people feel justified in and empowered by their biases and have no interest in changing them. The reality is that often our inherent subjectivity goes unchecked and can have horrific consequences.

DANGERS OF UNCHECKED SUBJECTIVITY

The 2012 Trayvon Martin–George Zimmerman case is a painful example of how unchecked biases can have fatal results. Trayvon Martin, a 17-year-old African American from Miami Gardens, Florida, was walking home from a convenience store with Skittles and a drink. George Zimmerman, a neighborhood watch volunteer, thought Trayvon was suspicious because he was black and was wearing a hoodie. George Zimmerman took matters into his own hands against the advice of the police and fatally shot Trayvon Martin. In 2013 George Zimmerman was subsequently acquitted of second-degree murder and of manslaughter charges, which ignited another conversation about race in this country. In response to the Zimmerman verdict, I wrote a blog in the *Huffington Post,* in which I shared my belief that pervasive societal mental models about young black men influenced the responses and behaviors of many of the people involved in the Trayvon Martin and George Zimmerman case. I believe that Zimmerman automatically judged that the young black man in a hoodie was up to no good. I believe that this unchecked bias drove his unwarranted behavior. In fact, I believe that Zimmerman's actions, the Sanford police department's response, and the jury's final verdict were all the consequence of unchecked subjectivity.

The challenge for us as a society is that our unchecked subjectivity often motivates discriminatory behavior that then becomes institutionalized and structural. We can clearly see how this has played out in our society over time. For example, mental models about African-American men have pervaded our society to such an extent that this segment of our population is clearly at risk, evidenced by the alarming drop-out, incarceration, and mortality rates. It is likely that these and other race, gender, sexual orientation, and religious disparities will persist until we, as human beings, grapple with our inherent subjectivity and begin to have a conversation about how to become more objective.

While our unchecked subjectivity can have profound consequences for groups of people, it can also be a business risk. Can leaders in business today afford to allow bias to inform their decision about customers, suppliers, or partners? If 75 percent of us are judging people unfairly at least once a month, what impact can that have on a business? What might it cost you as a leader?

Subjectivity, and the tendency to act based on unconscious biases, is a business risk that companies cannot afford to ignore. For example, there are many cases in which sales associates acted on their unconscious biases and made assumptions about the worthiness of a potential customer based on skin color. This famously happened in 2013 at a boutique in Zurich, where a salesperson rudely refused service to Oprah Winfrey. Obviously, the salesperson did not recognize Oprah and assumed that the black woman who showed interest in a $38,000 handbag could not afford it. This unchecked subjectivity cost the store $38,000 when Oprah walked out the door. It also cost them reputational capital because the incident went viral, and they were forced to publicly apologize. In another example, in 2013 Macy's, the department store, was accused of racial profiling by a number of black customers in its New York stores. Multiple customers said they were singled out and even detained after purchasing expensive merchandise, with the implication being that they were trying to shoplift. In August 2014 Macy's paid $650,000 to settle this dispute. The settlement came several days after Barneys New York agreed to pay $525,000 in fees and penalties following a nine-month investigation into a series of complaints from Barneys customers and former employees who claimed that door guards would exclusively single out minority customers and that in-store detectives would follow these customers as they walked around. Clearly, unconscious bias is a significant business risk and in these cases it can be quantified.

There are other situations equally harmful to businesses but may not be measurable. I recently worked with the new CEO of a private bank and investment management company to develop and facilitate a senior leadership meeting on objectivity. One of the key issues we discussed was that the profile of one of their key target wealth management customers, entrepreneurs, had changed. Their mental model was that successful entrepreneurs were white, male, and always dressed professionally in a suit and tie. The bankers all did. As a result, wealthy entrepreneurs who did not fit this profile were shunned and ultimately took their business to a more open-minded institution. The wealth management executives were losing market share in this segment, and they needed to rethink their assumptions about what successful entrepreneurs looked like, and how best to attract and service them.

In another example, Ken Chenault of American Express spoke at a 2013 leadership conference for The Partnership, a Boston-based nonprofit organization whose mission is to advance a new conversation about diversity. He talked about the importance of overcoming unconscious biases, and the need for American Express hiring managers to reevaluate and change their underlying assumptions about a key talent resource for their organization, IT professionals. His management team learned to adjust to the reality that many young professionals in technical fields may not present themselves conservatively, even if their skills are impeccable. They could no longer afford to evaluate talent based on unconscious biases and assumptions about appearance.

These are just a few examples of unconscious bias risk. What is this lack of objectivity costing your business: lost revenue, talent, or productivity? More importantly, how can businesses effectively mitigate this risk? To proactively address this issue as an objective leader, it is helpful to conduct an internal assessment of unconscious bias risk that may include the following:

1. Through focus groups and surveys, assess the level of employee engagement regarding inclusiveness, creativity, and innovation.
2. Measure interactions with customers through call center recordings and other customer feedback mechanisms.
3. Analyze the mix of customers to determine if the company is either losing share or not capturing share of specific demographic segments.
4. Assess the diversity of the supplier base.
5. Evaluate the strength of strategic partnerships, both domestically and globally if applicable, in terms of loyalty, price elasticity, and goodwill, and determine if unconscious bias is contributing to misunderstandings or distrust.

TRANSFORMING BIAS

Once your business has assessed its bias risk, the next step is to help your employees identify and transform their hidden biases. According to the research conducted by Margo J. Monteith, a social psychology professor at Purdue University, "the solution to automatic stereotyping lies in the process itself. Through practice, people can weaken the mental links that connect minorities to negative stereotypes and strengthen the ones that connect them to positive conscious beliefs."[5] As we have seen in the framework for increasing objectivity in the moment, the slight pause in the processing of a stereotype gives conscious, unprejudiced beliefs a chance to take over and allows for a more objective response. The question is whether or not you know your triggers for reacting to a person based on an unconscious bias. Do you feel uncomfortable in any way? Do you become tense, cautious when confronting a person against whom you have a bias?

To transform biases, to actually change the way you think and feel about a particular group of people, is similar to transforming other types of conscious and unconscious mental models. First, it requires an identification of the bias, which can be confirmed by the IAT test, followed by the process of transformational learning. Through knowledge, experiences, and feedback, you can shift a bias so that you are treating all people fairly and respectfully.

KNOWLEDGE: NEW WAYS OF THINKING

Without challenging our basic assumptions, we cannot increase objectivity and improve our relations with each other. As we have seen, it is new logic, a new line of reasoning that can help us create moments of insight to challenge our notions and transform the mental models that no longer serve us so that we can become more objective, and therefore more inclusive. The following Principle of Objectivity has proven to be effective in helping transform biases. It not only helps to improve our automatic responses to others, but can also shift the unconscious biases that lie beneath the surface.

PRINCIPLE 5: WE DID NOT CHOOSE OUR DIFFERENCES

Did you choose your skin color? Did you choose your gender? Did you choose your parents or their economic status? The answer to these questions, of course, is a resounding no. Then how can we, as human beings, judge and condemn ourselves and others based on something over which we have no control? The Human Genome Project has now proved beyond a shadow of a doubt that the number of genetic differences between even the two most distantly related humans is very tiny, roughly 0.1 percent of the total DNA. So what is the justification for the hatred and intolerance we have for other people who are mostly just like us, with a minor physical difference that they did not choose? How can we institutionalize how things ought to be for certain groups of people—what they should have access to, or what they deserve in terms of quality of life, access to education, health care, and other opportunities? Think about it! It is not inherently rational.

Unfortunately, as we have seen, many of us habitually compare ourselves with others to determine our own worth. Our mental model says that in order to feel good about ourselves, someone has to be "less than" us. And we begin that comparison with the most superficial aspects of ourselves. Is it possible that in order to feel better than others, and therefore good enough, we have judged and condemned groups of people who don't look or act like us?

Now, this line of reasoning does not in any way negate or diminish the history of suffering and discrimination that many groups of people have experienced. Rather, if framed correctly as an intolerable consequence of subjectivity, that history can be an integral component of the knowledge and experience required for transformative learning. Instead of feeling shame that you are a part of a group you did not choose that, sometime before you were born, discriminated against— or perhaps committed unspeakable atrocities against—members of another group, recognize that there is the potential for a moment of insight.

We talked about how the motivation to change is the most important part of transforming mental models that do not serve you. Perhaps the long history of discrimination, and the sense of injustice and disgust many of us often feel when confronted with the consequences of unchecked subjectivity, can become the catalyst for change instead of a reason for guilt or shame. The conversation then must shift to the reasons why acting on destructive biases no longer serves the person and why being more inclusive adds value to one's personal and professional life. As with all mental models, transforming biases can take time; but most importantly, it takes a desire and commitment to do so. The good news is that, according to the research, when given enough motivation, people may be able to teach themselves to inhibit prejudice so well that even their IAT test comes back clean.

To be an objective leader means not judging or categorizing others based on superficial differences that they did not choose. Being an objective leader means recognizing that there are societal mental models about skin color, race, gender, et cetera, that drive unjust responses that undermine creativity, inclusiveness, and collaboration. To be an objective leader means choosing to respond to "what is"—even though the person may look different, he or she will undoubtedly have a unique perspective and approach that will be valuable to the organization. And just as you want to be treated with respect and given the freedom to be who you are, being an objective leader means that you will grant all others—regardless of their appearance, their religion, or any other way that they are different from you—the freedom to be and to express who they are. Over time, you can create a new mental model based on this reality that will help you respond appropriately to every person you encounter.

EXPERIENCES INCLUDING COUNTERSTEREOTYPES

While motivation and commitment are key requisites to transforming bias, it is the neuroplasticity of the brain that allows us to make the shift. There have been many examples where people simply exposed themselves to positive images of the group against which they had bias, and the bias was indeed reduced. For example, when the race test is administered by a black man, test takers' *implicit bias toward blacks is reduced*. Having people think of black exemplars such as Barack Obama or Michael Jordan also lowered race bias scores. Interventions as brief as a few seconds had effects that lasted at least as long as 24 hours.

You can also support the process of shifting biases by creating counterstereotypes through new experiences with the group against which you may have a bias. Again, shifting requires that you, as the Subject, see things differently through new information, knowledge, lines of reasoning, and experiences that motivate you to refute the old biases. You find yourself thinking, *That is just not true! It never was!* Some have found great success by volunteering to work on a diverse team or expanding circles of friends outside of work. You may also consider participating in cultural events in your community, traveling abroad, or learning a new language. These are all effective ways to broaden your perspective about people who are not like you.

What is so compelling, and I have seen this in workshop after workshop, is that once you sit down and actually think through some of your underlying assumptions and bring those assumptions to your conscious awareness, it is nearly impossible to keep them. The light of your awareness alone destroys them. Then it becomes just a matter of breaking a habit, but as we know, sometimes breaking a habit can be difficult—though it can be done. Once you make the shift, you can rewire the brain consciously. Again, every time you interrupt that automatic reaction and respond differently, you are training your brain to fire differently.

Invariably, when people reflect on this individually and are then asked to share it with a partner, while there still may be a little shame there, most people are motivated to do the work to shift their behavior, to respond more objectively to people not like them. Most feel that, as with other mental models that were acquired, adopted, assimilated, and never questioned, they have the power to transform, to grow, to be more objective, to be a better person, to be a more effective leader.

Please remember, we were socialized with mental models that define for us how we see the world and how we relate to each other. We were taught as children that our measure of worth was relative to others—that someone had to be worse for us to be better. These are some of the mental models that have fueled conflicts and all forms of separatism around the world for ages. We were never taught that there is an objective reality that challenges and confronts many of the mental models that cause us to judge and condemn each other. These mental models have spiraled out of control, and humanity is now confronted with catastrophic probabilities.

To address these challenges, we must have the courage to question, unravel, and transform these mental models that have us trapped in separatism. Here is what we all can do:

- **Understand and accept our inherent subjectivity**. The fear and shame of being labeled a racist or another "-ist" evokes denial and rejection when, in reality, we all have bias. There is no shame or blame in having bias and stereotypical mental models that were formed when we were five years old, but as adults we are accountable for our responses, so we must be aware of and take control of our judgments and behaviors.

- **Learn and choose to increase our objectivity**. Once we understand and accept our inherent subjectivity, we must consciously choose to learn to see things as they are without projecting our own interpretations or assumptions, to seek to understand another person's perspective and to respond thoughtfully, deliberately, and appropriately to everyone we encounter.

- **Recognize our mental models and be open to the possibility that we may be wrong about what we believe**. We can begin to identify our mental models about race and other basis for difference by being aware of our triggers. For example, when we meet someone who is different from us, we can be aware if he or she evokes an uncomfortable physiological response, such as anger, fear, or anxiety. This could be an indication of an unconscious bias. By being aware of our mental models and biases, we can learn how to pause before we react automatically and subjectively, and we can choose to respond more thoughtfully and objectively. We must have the courage to question our behavior and our underlying assumptions and to develop new and more effective ways of understanding and interacting with all people, as well as situations and events.

- **Transform destructive and harmful mental models**. Once we are aware of our biases, we must choose to use our intellect to develop new ways of thinking, reasoning, and acting. We will continue to see outrageous displays of bias until we can come to grips with our inherent subjectivity and refute our belief that we are powerless to control our cognitive processes and our automatic reactions. We are not powerless over biases, mental models, and ways of thinking that can diminish ourselves or others and cause hurt, outrage, and divisiveness. Instead of being mindless, not questioning our assumptions, we can consciously choose our responses to everything we experience.

- **Change in response to new information**. As we saw earlier, with the brain's neuroplasticity, we all have this capacity. We all have the power to choose to respond objectively, to discern what is appropriate, what is right and proper, and to actually do it. Again, every time we interrupt our automatic reactions and choose a different response, we loosen those neural connections and create new pathways that can inspire inclusive and compassionate behavior toward all people.

- **Help minority youth overcome the mental models they confront each day**. Because our inherent subjectivity has gone unchecked for so long, and because there have been too many Trayvon Martins, we have all promulgated a vicious and dangerous cycle. We now know that other people's perceptions of us shape our self-concept. Therefore it is natural for our young minority children to project these circumstances onto themselves. Many adopt destructive mental models: "I will never make it," "The odds are against me, so why even try," or "I will either drop out of school, be racially profiled, go to jail, or die young." Because mental models are so powerful, more young minority men may slip through the cracks because they don't believe they have a choice. As adults, we do have a choice. We can change their experience by responding more objectively to our own experiences. We can also teach and empower young minorities, in fact all of our young people, with the knowledge that they do not have to accept or adopt other peoples' mental models about them. They have the power to defy the odds. They can choose to respond differently to what they confront and create new possibilities for their lives.

ACTION PLAN: EXERCISE 6

To help transform your biases, ask yourself the following questions and jot down your answers:

1. What thought or impression comes to mind when you see a member of a group against which you have a bias?
2. What is your behavior toward that person, generally?
3. How does it feel when you initially interact with that person? For example, are you apprehensive? Are you self-conscious about how you may be reacting?
4. How do you feel about your responses to that person?
5. Where did you get that thought or impression? When?
6. What mental model or stereotype may be driving that?
7. How long have you had this impression?
8. What is the basis for your judgment?
9. Is it true?
10. Is it fair?
11. Do you want to change your judgment and response to that person? Why?
12. What new or unbiased thoughts can replace the old thoughts?
13. What new information or line of reasoning do you need about that group that may help you shift your mental model?
14. What experience do you want to have to help you overcome this bias?

Chapter 8

MANAGING TEAMS AND ORGANIZATIONAL CHANGE

Objective leaders must understand that their effectiveness as a leader is directly related to the efficacy of their mental models—that is, how well those models drive their intended behavior. This may seem relatively straightforward, but it often is not. Leaders face several challenges when they are beginning to identify and evaluate their mental models in order to increase objectivity.

First, many leaders become frustrated when there is an organizational code for what it takes to be successful that directly conflicts with who they are as a person. For example, the company culture demands a 12–15 hour work day and working on weekends. For those with families, this is difficult. In other cultures, there is a social/networking component that is a key factor for success, yet for those who are shy or introverted, this can be uncomfortable. In response, leaders struggle to be something that they naturally are not. Conversely, sometimes personal mental models can undermine their ability to be an effective leader. For example, we might think of ourselves as inclusive and fair people, yet sometimes our unconscious biases cause us to respond in unexpected ways. Similarly, many of us imagine that effective leadership includes collaborating effectively, yet our personal mental models, such as the Control mental model, drive behavior that has the opposite effect. Another challenge for leaders is when unproductive organizational mental models, such as the competitive silo mentality, when certain departments or groups do not share information with others in the same company, undermine the ability to accomplish stated objectives. In the same vein, it can be problematic when a leader is facilitating the process of shifting an unproductive team mental model and a team member's personal mental model interferes. And finally, one of the greatest challenges for leaders is leading large-scale change initiatives, wherein the entire organizational culture must shift. In this chapter, we will review each of these leadership challenges and discuss how to overcome them.

ORGANIZATIONAL VERSUS PERSONAL MENTAL MODELS

Steve Ballmer, the former CEO of Microsoft, is a perfect example of a very successful leader who tried to change who he was to fit the role of head honcho. He behaved one way in his previous roles as senior vice president of sales and support, senior vice president of systems software, and vice president of marketing, behavior that people were accustomed to and responded well to. Once he became CEO, he developed a mental model that compelled him to become something that he wasn't. Rob Enderle described it in an article in *Datamation* this way: "Steve Ballmer had been the Microsoft Cheerleader when he got into the role of CEO, and you'd think that would have been a huge asset. But he largely gave up that duty and didn't really backfill himself, adopting a stuffy corporate personality that didn't seem to work for him or the firm. It was as if he tried to be what he thought a CEO should be and not what a CEO is. It was almost like he'd been cloned and the clone lost many of the skills that had made Ballmer so successful prior to becoming CEO: his passion, his candor, all seemed to evaporate over a few short years."[1] This might have been the beginning of his downfall as a CEO, which we revisit later.

This organizational versus personal mental model is also an issue for many women in the corporate world. The mental models we sometimes adopt for the new roles we play are often not effective. Some women have a mental model that they have to be domineering and cold in order to succeed. Unless this truly describes you, trying to be something you think others want is not sustainable. Not only will you not be happy, but your lack of authenticity is often obvious and ineffective. Similarly, a recent article by Deidre L. Redmond in the *Chronicle of Higher Education*, "A Black Female Professor Struggles with 'Going Mean,'" discussed the challenge of minorities and women in academia. Their mental model is that they "will not be granted the authority and respect of their male white counterparts unless they 'go mean,' become cold and I dare say angry."[2] As a result, some women and minority professors fundamentally transform their personalities in order to be successful.

To avoid this error, the first thing leaders must do is question their mental models before allowing assumptions to steer their behavior. In Ballmer's case, the relevant question would be, Is it true that you cannot both be yourself and be successful as a CEO? What is the evidence supporting this notion, and what is the evidence refuting it? To be an objective leader, you must ask yourself these questions when making assumptions. Is it true that women have to act differently to be successful? Is it possible that who you already are can, in fact, help you be more successful? Remember, objectivity is defined as seeing and accepting things as they are, including yourself. To be an objective leader, you must be able to see yourself clearly and value who you are, so that no matter what role you play, you are always yourself. If you find yourself in an environment where you cannot be yourself and be successful, I would challenge you to find an environment where you can.

PERSONAL MENTAL MODELS UNDERMINING LEADERSHIP EFFECTIVENESS

I recently coached the senior leadership team of a large, well-established medical center on how to increase team effectiveness through greater objectivity. The medical center was founded in 1972 and provides health services to an underserved community outside of Boston. I have rarely met such a dedicated group of leaders, all so passionate about their social mission. The six of them had been working together for a long time and trusted each other's commitment to the work. Sarah, the executive director, has been running the organization for over 30 years. She is a unique blend of intelligence, compassion, and efficiency. She cares about each member of her staff personally, and she is always looking for opportunities to improve staff communication and collaboration.

During my first meeting with the senior leadership team, it became very clear that Sarah's mental models had had a long-term impact on the overall effectiveness of the team. Their weekly meetings had become unproductive, with limited participation by the members of the team. The perception throughout the organization was that Sarah made all the decisions, and each member of the senior management team had to get Sarah's approval for everything. While it was obvious that they all had a profound connection to the work, they were not functioning as a senior management team should.

I started the process by asking each member of the senior management team to describe the mental model they have about the role they played in the organization. We started with Sarah, the executive director, who said her mental model is "I have to fix everything." As it turned out, this was her personal mental model that influenced everything she did. Michael, who ran the patient-centered team, said that his mental model was to be responsible for his department and make decisions. Sarah spoke up and said, "I want all of you to make your own decisions, and take the weight off of me." Janet, who supervised what was called the B team, spoke up and said that it didn't seem that way to her. Instead, she said, it seemed that Sarah preferred making her own decisions and not involving any of them in her process. Sarah was very surprised to hear that feedback. She replied that, from her perspective, she often asked for their opinions and was frustrated because no one responded. The team was surprised to hear that Sarah preferred more of their input and involvement. Darla, who was the head of call center operations, spoke up and said that when they gave her their opinion, they often didn't know whether it was considered and what the outcome was. Sarah said she could certainly change that. Emily, who ran the nursing department said that when she came to Sarah with a situation about one of her staff, she assumed Sarah did not trust her interpretation of the circumstances and wanted to talk to the involved people directly to make her own decision. Sarah responded that after 20 years of working together, she absolutely trusted Emily's assessment and did not want to talk to other people. Emily admitted that because of her own mental models, she was perhaps being defensive and was relieved to learn that the Sarah trusted her judgments.

Can you imagine how Sarah might have been feeling at this moment? Did she feel embarrassed? Did she feel unsupported, or even attacked by her staff? No, she did not. She was surprised, as we all were, that the first meeting was so open, so honest, so quickly. She openly acknowledged that, without her intention, her "I have to fix it" mental model compelled her to micromanage at times and gave her team the impression that she did not want their input. The team immediately saw how their individual mental models *and* their assumptions about each other were undermining their ability to collaborate effectively. Framed in the context of objectivity, we created a safe place where there was no reason for anyone to take anything personally. Michael spoke up and shared that he was delighted that their senior leadership team had made so much progress and that understanding other's perspectives was important. As a hard-charging, get-it-done type leader, he expressed concern that the process would take too long. "We don't have time for the warm and fuzzy stuff or having Kumbaya moments. We often have to act quickly depending on patient need." They all agreed. The key was to develop a way of communicating naturally that would be efficient in getting to understanding. Drawing on Peter Senge's Ladder of Inference, which was initially developed by Chris Argyris and subsequently presented in Senge's *The Fifth Discipline*, we came up with the following simple phrases to use in conversation with each other. These key phrases were based on the premise that the priority is not to push your agenda but to understand the other person: "Help me understand your thinking here." "What assumption or experience do you have that leads you to that conclusion?" "My assumption is that..." or "My interpretation of that was..." or "Was I correct in my assumptions that...?" "Am I understanding you correctly that...?" We all left the meeting feeling that communication in this way was doable and they were committed to practicing it.

And indeed, that meeting was the first of many more. Once everyone understood each other's mental models and which models were either supportive of or disruptive to the goal of effective collaboration, we began creating new processes and procedures to support the new model. For example, at one meeting we developed a framework for decision making. We asked each team member which decisions they were currently making, and which decisions they thought they should be making. In some cases, it was just a matter of empowering Ben, Sarah's executive assistant, to respond to specific senior management requests without checking with Sarah first. In other cases, it was as simple as copying certain people on e-mails. They developed a framework for when Sarah's involvement was required and when it was not, which empowered each member of the team. With the senior management team quickly becoming more collaborative, we wanted to support their respective teams as well. We identified an organizational mental model that seemed to impair overall teamwork throughout the organization. They call it the "hierarchy mental model," in which people at the lower rungs of the organization (the medical assistants) do not feel empowered to speak up because they feel their opinions will not be respected and valued. Perpetuating this model was that senior level staff (the doctors and department managers) did not seek out the opinions of lower-level staff (medical assistants and call center employees), instead looking only to their peers for input. Happily, the senior leadership team quickly recognized that given their mission, and the fact that every employee interacts with patients on some level, this model undermined their ability to deliver the best health care to the patient.

This particularly impacted Michael's patient-centered team. His team is organized around a holistic approach to patient care. The patient-centered team provides an array of health-care services to each patient based on their needs, through various professional providers. For example, a single patient might receive a routine medical exam, a flu shot, diabetes education and support, a nutrition consultation, mental health counseling, and family counseling, et cetera. This is where the hierarchy model can be so dangerous. The patient-centered team consists of doctors, psychiatrists, social workers, nurses, medical assistants, and intake/triage nurses and nurses' assistants, all interacting with and getting information about the same patient. However, because of the hierarchy mental model, Michael observed that the patient-centered team did not always communicate effectively. Michael clearly saw that facilitating the transformation of this mental model would help the team better understand the needs of the patient, better coordinate the plan for patient care, and achieve greater results for each patient.

It is imperative for you as a leader to understand organizational mental models and ways of thinking and interacting that may be undermining effectiveness. While there can be many reasons why people don't communicate effectively, it is often rooted in misunderstood assumptions and perceptions that are unrecognized and unchecked. In some organizations, such as medical centers and hospitals, the risks are too high. I admire Michael's leadership because he wanted to address this common issue *before* it resulted in the compromise of patient care.

SHIFTING UNPRODUCTIVE ORGANIZATIONAL MENTAL MODELS

Michael and I met and developed a plan to help shift his team's hierarchy mental model. Our approach was to raise the issue and inspire a conversation about how it may be impacting team collaboration and ultimately patient care. When the 20 members of the patient-centered team got together for the first time, we started with an icebreaker. I asked each person to share what they were most passionate about in their lives, something that people would not know about them, as well as what they enjoyed about working at the medical center. In order to shift unproductive team mental models, it is essential to build camaraderie and trust among team members. It is also important to build common ground around the positive aspects of working for the organization. Again, I was quite impressed to see that they bonded around the mission of helping other people. We ended the roundtable with Michael. A little uncomfortable with the softness of the meeting, Michael shared the things he enjoys most about working at the medical center. He then jumped right in and expressed his concern about the hierarchy mental model and how it was impacting patient care.

At first, people were defensive and said they did understand that other organizations had that problem. They did not want to admit that it was also happening at their medical center. Michael stepped in and said that yes, indeed, it is happening, but he thought they could change it together. As a leader you must be willing to openly but constructively point out the elephant in the room. In this case, people had just expressed that what they enjoyed most about working at the medical center was the people. Clearly they did not want to think they were not communicating effectively. This opened the way for people to talk more openly about the issues. Jim, a well-respected doctor, talked about a mistake he was making with a specific group of patients. He said he wished someone had pulled him aside to tell him that his actions and demeanor were unintentionally offending the patients. The feedback Jim received was that while many noticed it, they did not feel comfortable speaking up because he was a doctor. They made the assumptions that doctors do not want to be told they are wrong; they expected repercussions for speaking out. Jim assured them that if it were communicated appropriately, he would have been open and receptive to the feedback. They all agreed that their inability to openly communicate with each other could jeopardize the patient. The team also talked about the tendency of the team members with higher stature to make decisions without thinking about how it affected everyone else in the organization. Some team members interpreted that to mean that the impact on lower-level members of the organization was not as important, again reinforcing the mental model that lower-level employees do not have an equal voice and their voices are not valued.

To replace the hierarchy mental model, the team articulated a new approach they called the Full Engagement mental model, which states, "First priority will be the patient and everything we do will be centered around patient need. Everyone on the team has a unique and valuable perspective that must be shared with other team members in order to participate in and contribute to the patient plan for care. The team is integrated and interdependent and therefore when changes are made, impact at all levels of the organization must be evaluated, addressed, and communicated."

We then focused on identifying the actions that could be taken or changes that could be made at all levels of the organization to support this new mental model. For example, the team identified that in order for the mental model to work, they had to start with how they interacted during team meetings. They affirmed that to inspire others to be fully engaged, they needed to adopt a new way of communicating as well. They established that when someone participates and voices their opinion, there can be no judgment; that person must be acknowledged for their perspective, expertise, and contribution. We also focused on all the communications that needed to happen across the organization to cement and extend this new way of operating.

Finally, we developed a system for assessing progress. We agreed that we would allocate 15 to 20 minutes of the weekly meeting agenda to sharing experiences with the new mental model. The goal was to identify situations where it worked well; the improvement was noticed and appreciated. We also discussed situations where it broke down and the team reverted back to the old mental model.

Remember, when situations are intense and things are moving fast, which often happens in health-care organizations, sometimes we revert back to old ways of thinking and acting. The objective leader must closely examine those situations to determine if the gap between the new model and the old way of operating is structural or personal. If structural, it could mean that the mental model needs to be tweaked or adjusted in some way, or more processes or procedures must be implemented to support the new model. For example, to help people engage more in team meetings, Michael began e-mailing a recap of the discussion in the previous meeting along with the agenda for the upcoming meeting a few days ahead of time. In this e-mail he specifically requested that people think about and be prepared to share their perspective on the upcoming topics for discussion. If the gap was personal because an individual was unable to think and act through the new lens, it could mean that the new mental model was in conflict with a person's personal mental model. It is common that while a person clearly supports an organizational new mental model and understands why it is critical for the organization, their personal mindset may still prevent them from adopting the new model. For example, Justin, a nurse's assistant, struggled with the new Full Engagement mental model. While he believed it was important, his own mental model prevented him from adopting it. Justin was afraid of speaking up in meetings and confronting people directly with issues or concerns. In cases like this, the objective leader can support the employee in adopting the new model.

PERSONAL MENTAL MODELS IN CONFLICT WITH TEAM MENTAL MODELS

Helping people be more objective can be a rewarding aspect of leadership. The objective leader can learn to recognize when an employee's actions are inconsistent with that person's stated objectives. It is often a sign that the person has unconscious mental models driving their behavior. The key is to help the person identify the limiting mental model and create moments of insight and opportunities for transformation. It is important to start with the actions of the employee. The first step is acknowledgment. It is important for the employee to acknowledge, in this case, that the new Full Engagement mental model is important. Ask Justin: What do you think about our new model? What do you think the impact will be if we are all able to improve in this area? These are open-ended questions to help you uncover Justin's thoughts and feelings about the new team model.

The next step is recognition. In the spirit of nonjudgment and support, help the employee recognize that there is a gap between what needs to happen and what actually happened, and what the result is. Our tendency as leaders is to point out the problem and never ask why the employee did what they did. Ask Justin what happened. Let him describe the situation, how he was feeling, and what his response was. Focus on the feeling he had at the time. Often when someone is inconsistent, it's because they're anxious or afraid of doing what they know they should do. Ask him what would have been a preferred response based on the new team mental model.

The next step is identification. Ask Justin what his assumptions were at the time that prevented him from responding the way he wanted, in this case speaking up. It could be as simple as shyness, or it could be cultural. In some cultures it is frowned upon to speak up or talk back to elders. It could also be the Insecurity: "I'm not good enough" mental model. The key is to understand the personal mental models that were in conflict with the team mental model, and then, together, construct opportunities for that person to support the team model.

The final step is empowerment. You, as the leader, can teach each of your employees to be more objective. Specifically, you and the employee can develop a strategy for shifting the unproductive mental model, which means helping the employee discover that their old way of thinking is no longer valid or useful. For example, if it is a matter of feeling insecure about being ridiculed, it is not enough to say don't worry, that won't happen. The employee has to gain a moment of insight with new information and experience to shift the mental model. Your contribution is to help create experiences that refute the old mental model.

As we saw in Chapter 6, some of our unproductive mental models were formed when we were children. There may have been a strong emotional response to an experience and the associated assumptions, conclusions, and feelings then became hardwired in our neural nets. The experience may only have happened once, but it was powerful enough to become a dominant mental model. We never questioned it or examined whether it was still true or valid. We never stopped to look at how often we respond to situations through that same lens and what the impacts are. The goal here is: to help the employee reflect on the mental model and determine whether it still serves them with questions such as:

- How often do you see that mental model playing out?
- Is it possible that it was true in the past but is not true now?
- Do you think that developing a new way of thinking about it will serve you better in your job and career?

Once the employee understands that adopting the team mental model is important for his leadership development, the next step is for you to provide opportunities for growth. For example, perhaps instead of forcing Justin to speak up in meetings to support the team's mental model, encourage him to lead a smaller group discussion about a particular issue where he has expertise. Or invite him to send you his perspective on a particular issue, to be discussed at the next meeting. Once he receives your positive feedback and gains confidence, then agree to call on Justin at the meeting to participate. This may seem like hand-holding, but it really is just talent development. When you can support an otherwise talented employee to develop objectivity as a new leadership competency, it serves the entire organization—and of course, serves that person tremendously.

MANAGING LARGE-SCALE CHANGE INITIATIVES

Leaders must be able to manage change. The problem is that most change initiatives fail. In a series of exclusive interviews with Monica Langley of the *Wall Street Journal*, Steve Ballmer describes how his change effort met with so much resistance that it led him to conclude he should step down. It was sometime in 2012, during a contentious call with his board of directors, that Ballmer confirmed that the Microsoft board was not happy with his performance. While Microsoft was doing well in its traditional software business, it had missed epic changes in the industry, including Web-search advertising and the consumer shift to mobile devices and social media. The board was putting pressure on Ballmer to "reboot" and to accelerate change. He told the board he wanted to lead the charge and remain until his youngest son graduated from high school in four years. The board and he agreed that Ballmer would have to shake up the organization and refocus the business on future growth opportunities, such as mobile devices and online services. "The Directors 'didn't push Steve to step down,'" says Mr. Thompson, a longtime technology executive who heads the board's CEO-search committee, "but we were pushing him damn hard to go faster."[3] With this much pressure, Ballmer knew that his reboot plan would require a complete corporate overhaul. For guidance, he called his longtime friend, Ford's Mr. Alan Mulally, who had great success turning around Ford through teamwork and simplifying the Ford brand. "It was a wake-up call for Mr. Ballmer, who had run the software giant with bravado and concedes that 'I'm big, I'm bald and I'm loud.' He realized that over the past 33-plus years he had helped build Microsoft's culture, which included corporate silos where colleagues were often pitted against one another—a competitive milieu that spurred innovation during Microsoft's heyday. However, now this culture sometimes left groups focused on their own legacies and bottom lines rather than on the big technology picture and Microsoft as a whole. He recalls thinking: 'I'll remake my whole playbook. I'll remake my whole brand.' So Ballmer jumped in...quickly."[4]

The problem was that large-scale teamwork was not part of Ballmer's mental model, nor was it a part of the organization's mental model or culture. His attempt to change both his personal and organizational mental model so abruptly caused immediate resistance. For example, his leadership mental model, which everyone had already adapted to, was that he consulted with Microsoft's unit chiefs individually, often directing and demanding results. Under the new teamwork mental model, he began inviting them to sit together in a circle in his office to foster camaraderie. "It was a radical change in his leadership style and was a lurching corporate-culture change. 'It's not the way we operated at all in Steve's 30-plus years of leadership of the company,' says Mr. [Satya] Nadella, an executive vice president. In another example, Qi Lu, an executive vice president, submitted a 56-page report on applications and services. Mr. Ballmer sent it back, insisting on just three pages—part of a new mandate to encourage the simplicity needed for collaboration. Mr. Lu says he retorted: 'But you always want the data and detail!' Mr. Ballmer admitted that his senior team struggled with the New Steve. Some resisted on matters large—combining engineering teams—and small, such as weekly status reports."[5]

"Mr. Ballmer says he started to realize he had trained managers to see the trees, not the forest, and that many weren't going to take his new mandates to heart. In May 2013, he began wondering whether he could meet the pace the board demanded: 'No matter how fast I want to change, there will be some hesitation from all constituents—employees, directors, investors, partners, vendors, customers, you name it—to believe I'm serious about it, maybe even myself,' he says. At the board's June meeting in Bellevue, Washington, Mr. Ballmer says he told the directors: 'While I would like to stay here a few more years, it doesn't make sense for me to start the transformation and for someone else to come in during the middle."[6] Steve Ballmer retired from Microsoft, effective August 21, 2014.

We can certainly admire Ballmer for his accomplishments over a 33-year career with Microsoft. In this next section we will highlight several key lessons we can learn from what has been reported about Ballmer's experience that will help you approach large-scale change initiatives such as this with greater objectivity.

CHANGE INITIATIVE: PEOPLE

John P. Kotter, in his article *Leading Change: Why Transformation Efforts Fail*, says one of the top reasons change initiatives fail is because "executives underestimate how hard it can be to drive people out of their comfort zones."[7] As we have seen, so much of what we do in the workplace is automatic. At every level of the organization, from executive leadership to individual contributors, how we interact in meetings, how we interact with the boss, how we run meetings, how we manage others, and how we communicate has become routinized and part of what we expect. We have become quite comfortable with our patterns of behavior in the workplace. The problem is that our brains have a very strong protective mechanism that, with intense bursts of neural firing, alerts us to "errors," which neuroscientists call perceived differences between expectation and reality. So, even when we try to make the slightest change in our routines, there is often a feeling of discomfort or in some cases panic. David Rock and Jeffrey Schwartz, in their article "The Neuroscience of Leadership," describe it this way: "Try to change another person's behavior, even with the best possible justification, and he or she will experience discomfort. The brain sends out powerful messages that something is wrong, and the capacity of higher thought is decreased. Change itself thus amplifies stress and discomfort; managers (who may not from their position in the hierarchy perceive the same events in the same way that subordinates perceive them) tend to underestimate the challenges inherent in implementation."[8] It is no wonder that Ballmer's senior leadership team resisted. They were not just asked to change one thing that had become automatic; they were being asked to forget everything they learned about how to successfully operate at Microsoft. All of the rules had changed, and there was no new playbook. It must have been disorienting. Leaders of change initiatives must understand that change can be uncomfortable and disorienting and the impact of change on morale, even under the best circumstances, cannot be underestimated.

CHANGE INITIATIVE: BUILDING AND DEVELOPING A TRANSFORMATION TEAM

Although it doesn't sound like Ballmer had much choice since he was constantly being pressured to accelerate change, the first step in leading a change initiative is to build a transformation team to design and manage the change process. It is critical, if you are charged with leading the change, that you gain the active participation and commitment from the leaders of all the functional areas in the company. In your first meeting with your transformation team, be candid about the challenges and/or the opportunities the organization is facing, and establish a sense of urgency. Your objective at this first meeting is for every leader to understand how important it is for the organization to change. The current state and the end state must be clearly defined. Each leader must believe and be able to articulate "this is where we are now, our current state, but this is where we need to be, the end state or desired state." In the Microsoft case, the software business was performing well, but Microsoft wanted to become a key provider of devices and services for businesses and individuals.

The next step is to establish protocols for engagement. The transformation team must first discover the underlying assumptions or mental models about the desired state or transformation process. The team leader should invite the team members to voice their assumptions. The leader should establish the rule that no one is to comment immediately on what is being expressed; the goal is to get everything on the table without judgment. This is where initial resistance can be addressed, but more importantly, this is where the leader of the change initiative can lead the team through an objective process for evaluating assumptions. It is natural for members of the transformation team, at this early stage, to express assumptions such as:

- "I think we will lose key people if we try to make this change."
- "Our people don't have the skill sets required to make this change."
- "Other companies have tried to change in this way and failed."
- "The burden of the change will fall on my team."
- "We will have to establish a whole new set of procedures and policies, and we won't have time for that."

It is important that you, the leader, spend as much time on this as possible and capture all the assumptions on a white board. Then for each assumption, ask these questions: What leads you to that conclusion? What is the confirming evidence, and does evidence exist to the contrary? Is this assumption valid, and does it point to an issue that we will need to address going forward? What is a new way of thinking about this issue that may support our initiative? The goal here is for the transformation team to establish a method of communication in which concerns and assumptions are addressed throughout the change process. Once the transformation team learns how to approach the process objectively by identifying and evaluating their own underlying assumptions and identifying new ways of thinking and acting to support the end state, the next step is to broadly identify the organizational mental models that support the new initiative and those that are disruptive.

CHANGE INITIATIVE: IDENTIFYING ORGANIZATIONAL MENTAL MODELS

Just like our personal mental models drive our responses to everything we experience, organizational mental models dictate how people interact with each other, how work gets done, what behaviors are valued, and what constitutes success. Most people adopt personal mental models about their work based on the mental models they perceive in the organization. As we discussed earlier, sometimes this is comfortable, sometimes not, but either way, the employee has routinized a way of thinking and acting to adapt to the culture of the organization. Change cannot happen successfully unless these mental models are identified, evaluated, and then reinforced or transformed. For example, in the case of Microsoft, it was clear that their culture of competitive silos instilled behaviors in many of their employees that was disruptive to the corporate change initiative.

The transformation team must therefore develop approaches to strengthen, support, and leverage the existing organizational mental models that support the new initiative. In addition, for those organizational mental models that are in conflict with the desired state, it is important to begin a process of transforming the mental model as we reviewed earlier in this chapter. In the case of Microsoft, Ballmer conceded that the existing culture of corporate silos and competition made people resist the new Steve and his new organizational mental model of teamwork. The collaboration and trust between employees and groups that was required for a successful corporate overhaul was not there. While many probably supported the new model in theory, each had constructed their own personal mental models based on the existing culture, and there did not appear to be a focus on or time allocated to addressing this issue.

CHANGE INITIATIVE: CONSTRUCTING THE CAPABILITIES AND MILESTONE MAP

It is unfortunate that Microsoft's board put so much pressure on Ballmer to go faster. In addition to underestimating the difficulty of driving people from their comfort zones, another key reason why change initiatives fail, according to Kotter, is that "managers don't realize transformation is a process, not an event, and it can take years. Pressure to accelerate the process undermines success."[9] Leaders of change initiatives should try not to think in terms of time. If the mental model underlying the process is that we have to change quickly, there will be a focus on getting the quick result versus getting the best result. Remember, when the pressure to perform intensifies and the stakes are high, we don't see things as they are. Instead of thinking about time, think in terms of steady progress and milestones. Once the transformation team has defined current state and end state and has identified the organizational mental models that support or disrupt the end state, the next step is to construct a capabilities and milestones map. Below is an example of a map that can be used to record and communicate the process.

The left side of the capabilities and milestone map should clearly define the current state of the overall organization, in terms of revenues, market position, innovation, competitive advantage, et cetera. It is also important to identify the current organizational mental models, the way works gets done and people and teams interact. On the right side of the map should be specific components of the end or desired state, including the required organization mental models to support it. In the middle of the map, the transformation team, without the constraint of time, should think through and create a list of the capabilities the organization must have in order to meet the demands of the marketplace throughout the change process. The team should establish milestones and end-state goals for the organization as a whole and then specifically for each department. For example, if the IT infrastructure has to be upgraded to achieve the end state, it is important to clearly define and visibly display on the Capabilities and Milestone Map the critical capabilities that must

Objective Change Initiative Capabilities and Milestone Map		
Current State	**Capabilities & Milestones**	**End State**
ORGANIZATION	ORGANIZATION	ORGANIZATION
◆ Who we are and where we are today	❑ List capabilities that must be maintained throughout change process	◆ Who we want to be and where we want to go
◆ Organizational Mental Models: • Supportive of or disruptive to change	❑ Identify milestones, metrics, when and how to communicate	◆ Organizational Mental Models required to sustain end state
Functional Department: ◆ What is the current state of the department? ◆ What are the department's mental models? • Supportive of or disruptive to change	Functional Department: ❑ What are the mission's critical processes and functions required to support the organization? ❑ What are the specific, measurable, milestones to monitor and report to ensure continuity throughout process?	Functional Department: ◆ What is the desired state of the department to support the end state of the organization? ◆ What are new mental models the department needs to get there?
Operating Principles: When efforts do not produce the desired results, it is an opportunity to learn, to strengthen mental models or improve processes, not a failure. Communicate progress in measurable terms and celebrate progress in meaningful ways.		

be maintained. Each member of the team should be assigned responsibility for oversight of their specific areas of change. It is important to understand that not only does organizational transformation take time, but the design of the process of transformation also takes time. It is critical that enough time is allocated to designing this process.

CHANGE INITIATIVE: COMMUNICATION

When the transformation team completes its design of the process, the next step is to communicate the strategy for change throughout the organization. This is critical. Each member of the transformation team must go back to their organizations and engage their teams in the process of transformation. Each senior leader must communicate the challenges and opportunities to their teams in a way that invites them to own and participate in the process. The transformation team has already identified the changes in mental models that will be required to achieve the desired state. The goal of each transformation team member, then, is to try to cultivate moments of insight within his own organization so that employees choose to modify their mental models to support the change. For example, as a member of the transformation team, the head of IT meets with his team and presents them with the current state and also the milestones and end-state goals for their department. The head of IT should start the tactical design process with this team by identifying and evaluating underlying assumptions that support or disrupt the work of the team in achieving their end-state objectives. The IT leader then engages his team in a process of designing the specific activities, processes, and procedures their team will need to implement in order to achieve milestone goals and end-state goals.

CHANGE INITIATIVE: MONITORING AND REPORTING PROGRESS

This final step is key. Change initiatives are fluid, with many variables: some are predictable, some are uncontrollable, and some are unknowable.

Monitoring progress therefore becomes a test in objectivity. Our tendency is to expect specific results from the actions we take. Our assumption is that if we did not achieve the desired result, then we failed. The transformation team must adopt a principle that when things do not produce the desired result, it is an opportunity to learn, to strengthen mental models or improve processes, not a failure. In the early stages, when people are in the process of adopting new ways of thinking and acting, their old mental models can still influence behavior. Even after a moment of insight, if the change process is met with perceived failure, it weakens the resolve of the employees and can undermine the whole process. It is important then to define broad but measurable and visible milestones. Once achieved, milestones and progress should be communicated and celebrated. For example, early on when Ballmer was trying to achieve a large-scale mental model shift from a silo mentality to a teamwork mentality, it might have been helpful to task teams with broad goals and publicly recognize and reward the team for achieving them. This would have reinforced the new mental model and inspired others to have moments of insight.

Change initiatives do not have to be painful, and they certainly don't have to fail or yield less than the desired result. If the leader can approach the process with more objectivity, it can actually be an effective vehicle to develop talent and create highly effective leaders poised to confront the ongoing challenges and opportunities in the marketplace. Exercise 7 leads you through a process to understand and transform the mental model of your team in order to improve team collaboration.

ACTION PLAN: EXERCISE 7

THE OBJECTIVE LEADERSHIP AND TEAM COLLABORATION

The first step is to understand the existing team mental models by setting the stage and establishing common ground.

- Beginning with you, each person is asked to share something about themselves that people may not know; something that they are passionate about and what they like most about their job or the company
- Educate the group that everyone has mental models about their job and the team
- Share your mental model about your role as leader
- Ask each team member to share their mental model about their role

DEVELOPING A NEW TEAM MENTAL MODEL FOR COLLABORATION

- Beginning with you, share your vision or mental model about team collaboration and effectiveness
- Ask each person to share their mental model about effective team-work
- With everyone's input, identify, clearly articulate, and build consensus for a new team mental model—write it down!

TRANSFORMING TEAM MENTAL MODEL

- What are the obstacles to creating this new way of thinking and acting?
- What behaviors or ways of thinking are disruptive to the new model?
- What personal mental models about my job or my role may I need to rethink in order to support the new model?
- What new skills or processes do we need to overcome the obstacles?
- What behaviors and actions are supportive to the new mental model?
- How do we measure progress?
- How do we know when we are adopting the new model? What are the indicators of success?
- What is our process for tweaking our new team mental model based on progress?

Part V

THE OBJECTIVE
ENTREPRENEUR

Chapter 9

THE OBJECTIVE LEADER AND THE ASPIRING ENTREPRENEUR

We now know that the way a person frames their world—what they think about themselves, others, and the world around them—will influence their experience in all aspects of their lives. Regardless of what career they choose, everyone's success or failure depends on their mental models and how they respond to the opportunities and challenges they confront each day. The more objective they can be, the greater their chances for sustained success and happiness.

We have also learned that it is harder to be objective about a person, situation, or event in which one is emotionally invested. If one's self-concept, personal security, or belief system is connected to the person, situation, or event, it is difficult to see things clearly. While this is true for most people in general, it is nearly impossible for entrepreneurs. Because they are often driven by their unyielding passions, many entrepreneurs have a great deal at stake, personally, when they start a business. Some don't want to work for anyone else anymore. In fact, many people in corporate positions get fed up with working for someone else. They are tired of the politics that often exist in corporate environments and consider entrepreneurship as a viable career path. Many start businesses on the side because they want to be independent and self-sufficient. And in the beginning, most actually like wearing all the hats. They like being the boss. But at some point, when it is time to take the leap and focus on the business full time, they face the reality that there is no more paycheck coming in, and now they are their own bottom line. If they have a family, there is an added level of emotional investment; the family's livelihood depends on how well they perform. Many toss and turn at night wondering, *Am I doing the right thing, or am I bankrupting my family?*

With all of this going on, is it really possible for an aspiring entrepreneur to be objective? Can entrepreneurs balance passion with objectivity? I learned the hard way that emotional investment can fuel subjectivity, which, left unchecked, can limit your ability to see things as they are and make good decisions. It is therefore especially critical for people considering entrepreneurship to first identify and evaluate their mental models, their underlying assumptions about themselves, others, the world, and, of course, the entrepreneurial process. Aspiring entrepreneurs must clearly understand the lens through which they perceive, think, and act so that they are making sound judgments and smart decisions about their venture.

As we have seen, mental models are deep-rooted ideas and beliefs about the way things are and the way things ought to be. These mental models become the basis for how we perceive, interpret, and respond to everything we experience. It is important to emphasize "perceive." As we said earlier, our beliefs about how things are or ought to be are so powerful that they can alter perception itself; we just won't see or hear what's obvious to everyone else. Recently I was working with Constance, who is married with no children and working at a pharmaceutical company. Constance had started a line of women's blouses. She had achieved proof of concept for her line, which means that she had established distribution in a few small retailers and customers were buying her products.

She was now pursuing larger retailers for her line. The retailer's director of vendor management responded to the entrepreneur's letter of inquiry with an e-mail, which clearly stated that the buyer was not looking for any new items but they appreciated learning more about her business. The entrepreneur was so excited. She actually interpreted that to mean that the retailer was interested in her product, which was not true. It may be hard to believe, but Constance is one of the most well-regarded leaders in her field. On the job, she always evaluates situations clearly, makes the most effective decisions, and is constantly being promoted to new levels of responsibility. Yet when it comes to her own business, Blouses by Constance, her passion project, she has blinders on.

Vincent, another early stage entrepreneur who is widely recognized as a very talented designer of men's accessories with excellent relationship management skills, was absolutely thrilled when he became a vendor of a major retailer. But with limited cash flow, a small team, and other obstacles, the entrepreneur struggled to meet the terms of the retail buyer. Although his product was selling in ten of the retailer's locations, things finally came to a head, and the buyer informed the entrepreneur that his accessories would be discontinued and that he would not receive an order for the fall season. The entrepreneur clearly understood what the buyer was saying and was very disappointed. Later, he asked his mentor if he should send the buyer samples for the upcoming fall season. Remember, objectivity is seeing and accepting things as they are. In this case an extremely talented, creative, competent, and hardworking entrepreneur, whom people believed in, could not accept things as they were and kept hoping that something would change. Again, it may not seem rational, yet it's incredibly common. In my own case, I could not even contemplate the idea that my supplier would terminate the relationship with their top distributor, which represented 75 percent of sales. After all, it wasn't rational—at least it wasn't to me. I was wrong.

The goal of this chapter is to help you evaluate entrepreneurship as a career path by exposing you to the latest thinking about the entrepreneurship process and how successful entrepreneurs really think and act. We will debunk the common myths about the entrepreneurial process. Much of the common wisdom about the process has changed in the last ten years. We will review the latest research and methodologies that will help you reframe the way you think about the entrepreneurial process and help you develop new mental models upon which to approach your venture. Given this new understanding, we will then review the five most common mental models, first identified in Chapter 6, and explore how they can undermine entrepreneurs. We will explore new ways of thinking and acting that can help the aspiring entrepreneur overcome these limiting mental models.

DEBUNKING THE MYTHS

Aspiring entrepreneurs have heard many myths about the entrepreneurial process. These myths, if believed, become the basis for mental models about what it means to be a successful entrepreneur. To help you evaluate the entrepreneurial process clearly, we will review the most common myths such as the following:

MYTH 1: IF I AM SUCCESSFUL IN MY JOB WHERE I MANAGE PEOPLE, I WILL BE SUCCESSFUL AS AN ENTREPRENEUR.

This is not true. Based on Saras Saraswathy's groundbreaking book *Effectuation: Elements of Entrepreneurial Expertise*, we now know that corporate leaders and entrepreneurs rely on two different approaches, or logics, to thinking and acting. Individual contributors, managers, and senior leaders of corporations tend to lead with and rely on a causal or predictive logic, which states that "to the extent that we can predict the future, we can control it."[1] This approach to thinking and acting is based on the following principles:

- Goals are predetermined and achievable given known information.
- Enough information is known for rigorous analysis and testing.

- Tools and frameworks are available to guide decision making.

- Optimal solutions are identifiable within a given set of constraints.

- Through analysis, risk can be minimized or mitigated to achieve optimal returns.

- Outside organizations are seen as competitors and barriers to the future.[2]

Business planning, project management, risk analysis, and financial forecasting are all traditional business processes based on the assumption that we can predict the future from our past experiences.

The most successful entrepreneurs lean toward a very different logic. "It is a creative logic, which states: to the extent we can control the future, we do not need to predict it."[3] Saraswathy interviewed 245 US entrepreneurs that had at least 15 years of entrepreneurial experience and had started multiple companies—both successes and failures, with revenues between $6.5 million and $200 million—and had taken at least one company public. She concluded that the most successful entrepreneurs engage in a creative process of "act, learn, repeat." Most entrepreneurs that she interviewed started with a broad goal in mind, and they took action based on the best information and resources available at the time. Then, without preconceived notions or assumptions, they objectively evaluated the results of those actions. Based on what they learned from the analysis of the previous action, they acted again. This process is repeated: act, learn, repeat. The entire entrepreneurial process is therefore a process of discovery and an act of creation. While the use of a predictive logic has its place in the entrepreneurial process, successful entrepreneurs prefer to create rather than predict. So, if you are currently a leader in a corporation, it is likely that you have mental models about how to respond to business challenges in an organization. This is often based on a predictive logic. To become a successful entrepreneur, you must develop new mental models about thinking, acting, managing, and leading. To help you reframe your mental model, ask yourself the following questions before starting a venture.

- How easily can you shift your logic from predictive to creative?
- How comfortable are you with uncertainty?
- How creative can you be about what action to take without preconceived notions?
- How empowered are you to take action when the results of your actions are unknown?
- How objective can you be in evaluating results and choosing the next step when your initial results are not what you expected?

MYTH 2: SUCCESSFUL ENTREPRENEURS MUST WRITE A BUSINESS PLAN BEFORE LAUNCHING THEIR COMPANIES.

No, they do not. In fact, even the concept of a launch has changed. Of the CEOs interviewed by Saraswathy, 60 percent had not written a business plan, and only 12 percent had done market research in the traditional way.[4] Instead of launching a venture based on the predictive logic of a business plan, the most successful entrepreneurs refine their idea as they act and learn in an ever-evolving process of objective discovery. The goal is to discover a business model that is repeatable and scalable. Instead of a business plan, many entrepreneurs use process maps and guides such as Alex Osterwalder and Yves Pigneur's *Business Model Canvas* to discover the key components of the business model.[5] With this map, entrepreneurs establish a hypothesis about each of the nine components of a business model and then take action to test the hypothesis. Essential to this discovery process is a willingness to "pivot," to know when to shift gears and go in a different direction. Eric Ries, a tech entrepreneur and author of *The Lean Start-up*, says, "Through pivots, we can build companies where the failure of the initial idea isn't the failure of the company."[6]

Once the entrepreneur discovers a differentiated, repeatable, and scalable business model and needs capital to execute, *then* the entrepreneur might develop a business plan. Comprehensive business plans that include market research and pro forma financial statements are primarily used for raising capital. Whether it be traditional forms of capital such as debt from banks, community development financial institutions, micro-lenders, or equity capital from angel investors and venture capitalists, a well-thought-out business plan is required. Even nontraditional funding sources of capital such as crowd funding will require some version of a written business plan.

MYTH 3: TO BE A SUCCESSFUL ENTREPRENEUR, I HAVE TO THINK OF AN IDEA THAT NO ONE ELSE HAS EVER THOUGHT OF.

Absolutely not. First, it is very unlikely that you will think of something that no one has ever thought of. In fact, you can reasonably assume that others have thought of your idea. Underlying this myth is a common fear among entrepreneurs. In all of my classes at Babson, at least one student will ask, "How can I prevent someone from stealing my idea?" My answer: "Entrepreneurship is about execution. Many people may have a similar idea but will not act, they will not execute. The question is, how passion-ate are you about your idea, and how hard will you work to shape the opportunity to create value? Once you have shaped the opportunity, and have developed a prototype or other form of intellectual property that can be patented, then, of course, protect it, but many ideas are not patentable at all. For most ideas, it comes down to execution. So, let's take that off the table."

The best business ideas are often the simple ones that aim to solve a problem or fill a need. Innovative entrepreneurs are always asking how something can be better or what would fix a certain problem. Secondly, because the entrepreneurial process is a journey of discovery, successful entrepreneurs skip the traditional idea generation or brainstorming proc-esses and start with what they already have. The successful entrepreneurs interviewed by Saraswathy had a means-driven orientation, as opposed to the goal-driven orientation of the corporate leader. In fact, she thinks of expert entrepreneurs as head chefs who thrive when given a rather pitiful assortment of ingredients and are challenged to create something a customer would want to eat. Corporate leaders, by contrast, decide they are going to make lasagna, so they make a list and go shopping. They come back and begin a clearly defined process of chopping, measuring, mixing, and preparing the lasagna in the most efficient, cost-effective manner possible. The creative entrepreneurial process "does not begin with a specific goal. Instead, it begins with a given set of means and allows goals to emerge contingently over time from the varied imaginations and diverse aspirations of the founders and the people with whom they interact."[7]

The question then is: What are your means? What are the ingredients that you have with which you can create? Successful entrepreneurs ask themselves the following questions.

Who am I? What are my unique gifts and talents? About what am I most passionate? Being objective about your core strengths and how they can be leveraged to create value is the first place to start. Am I a good speaker? Am I a creative designer? Am I a good cook? Am I a good teacher? Am I analytical by nature? Do I like engaging with people? Who am I?

What do I know? In addition to understanding who you are, it is important to assess what you know, both professionally and personally. Many people start ventures because they have been successful working for someone else in a certain industry and have identified a gap in the market or a customer need that is not being met. Others start ventures by identifying a problem in the field in which they have subject matter expertise. Ask yourself: What is my field of expertise? What professional experiences have I had? On a personal level: What are my hobbies? What do I know the most about based on my personal experience? What has had the greatest impact on me? As we have seen, we all have unique gifts and talents, and as entrepreneurs we should start there. In addition, we all have unique circumstances and experiences that have shaped who we are and what we know. Therefore entrepreneurs must objectively assess their talents and also what they gained from their circumstances and experiences that gives them a unique skill set, area of expertise, or unique perspective on the world upon which to create. For example, I currently coach an entrepreneur that has been surrounded by diabetes since she was a child. Her grandmother had it, her father has it, and her uncles, aunts, and many of her friends' parents are struggling to manage the disease. She has observed the frustration and difficulty of her loved ones trying to find tasty foods to maintain their health. She is now using her experience and concern for her family as the basis to discover an opportunity to combat diabetes in her country with a new line of healthy snack foods that can lower blood sugar. Being an objective entrepreneur requires that you leverage all that you are, and all that you know, in order to create value.

MYTH 4: WHEN I START MY BUSINESS, I HAVE TO WEAR ALL THE HATS, DO EVERYTHING MYSELF.

This is no longer true. In fact, The Global Entrepreneurship Monitor Massachusetts 2010 Report reveals that building a team is a critical first step in the entrepreneurial process. Solo entrepreneurs are less successful than entrepreneurs that have a team. It was found that "the majority of both early-stage (58 percent) and established businesses (82 percent) were started by a single founder. This means that the majority of entrepreneurs are starting and running their businesses alone. However, early-stage businesses were more likely than established firms to be started and run by a team of founders, which is a positive sign, as research suggests that businesses started and run by teams are more likely to have long-term success."[8]

This makes sense because it is almost impossible to scale your business without the support of people with specific areas of expertise. Vincent, the men's accessory entrepreneur who lost his relationship with the major retailer now looks back and feels that his biggest mistake was not building a team. He couldn't do it all himself, and the retailer ultimately lost faith in his company's ability to meet the vendor requirements.

So far, you have assessed your means and taken stock of who you are and what you know. The next step is to consider who you know.

Successful entrepreneurs engage others in their idea at the very beginning. They think about everyone they know both professionally and personally. A good way to start this process is to write down the names of the people in your industry or work that you admire either for who they are or for what they know. For example, if it is someone you admire because of his or her work ethic, patience, and compassion, or subject matter expertise, jot the name down. If you admire someone's creativity and ability to think differently, add that name to your list. If you have determined that you are great at product design but not very good at sales and marketing, think about people you know that have sales and marketing skills. Many entrepreneurs who have an idea for a business are not necessarily good at operations or financial management. While you are working on tweaking the product to deliver the maximum value to the customer, you may need someone on your team who can manage the supply chain, manufacturing, and distribution processes. In addition, you may need someone to crunch the numbers to make sure your business can be profitable.

Once you have identified contacts that could add value to your business, the next step is to enroll them in your vision. Enroll means commitment by you *and* them. These people are often called self-selected stakeholders, which means that they are committing their knowledge and resources to the venture. As you build a team of self-selected stakeholders, your means will change. You not only have who you are, what you know, and who you know, you now have who *they* are, what *they* know, and who *they* know. Leveraging the strengths, knowledge, and resources of self-selected stakeholders also helps reduce your risk.

MYTH 5: TO BE TRULY PASSIONATE ABOUT MY BUSINESS, I HAVE TO RISK EVERYTHING.

I certainly thought so, which is why I ended up losing so much. And I wasn't the only one getting that message. Ten to fifteen years ago there were computer-based entrepreneurship training simulations based on the mental model that if the entrepreneur was not willing to risk everything—their current salaries, their savings, and even their mother's house—they were not serious enough to be successful. (Therefore, they never "won" the simulation.) Even now, while lenders and equity investors don't expect entrepreneurs to risk it all, they still demand so-called "skin in the game." The successful entrepreneur understands this, and makes a conscious choice about the amount of risk he or she is willing to take on. Saraswathy calls this the principle of affordable loss. In other words, successful entrepreneurs see their venture as an opportunity to explore: "They determine how much they are willing to lose and leverage limited means in creative ways to generate new ends and means."[9] Ask yourself the following questions: How much money am I willing to lose to explore this opportunity? If I were a potential investor in my business, how much would I be willing to invest based on an objective assessment of my idea and team? Conversely, successful entrepreneurs must also evaluate their opportunity costs. Ask yourself: If I leave my job to focus on my business, what will that cost me—in lost salary, stature in the organization, reputation, et cetera? How much of these things am I willing to lose? And lastly, successful entrepreneurs decide up front how much they are willing to risk personally. How many Little League games are you willing to miss? How many date nights with your significant other are you willing to "rain check"? To what degree are you willing to change and potentially hurt your relationships with your friends and family? These are critical questions. An objective entrepreneur, who sees things as they are, asks these questions—not just once in the beginning, but also at key milestones along the way.

MYTH 6: ACCESS TO CAPITAL IS THE NUMBER ONE REASON WHY BUSINESSES FAIL.

The failure rate of small businesses is hard to nail down. According to Bloomberg, eight out of ten businesses will fail within the first 18 months. Fasal Hoque, in his 2012 Fast Company article entitled *Why Most Venture Backed Companies Fail*, cites research by Harvard Business School's Shikar Ghosh. "Ghosh's research indicates that as many as 75 percent of venture-backed companies never return cash to investors, with 30 to 40 percent of those liquidating assets where investors lose all of their money. His findings are based on research of more than 2,000 venture-backed companies that raised at least $1 million from 2004 to 2010."[10] Why so high? While running out of cash and access to capital tops most of the lists of why businesses fail, it isn't that simple. There is often more to it than that. What are the decisions and underlying assumptions of the entrepreneur that contributed to the problem in the first place?

LESSON LEARNED

In my case, when it took longer than eight weeks for the product to arrive from South Africa, I chose to order more inventory so that I would not run out of inventory for my customers. Ordering and warehousing more inventory then made it difficult to sell through enough product to meet the payment terms. It got to a point where I was always out of cash, and ultimately my distribution agreement was terminated because of nonpayment, although it turns out that was not the only reason. I assumed the supplier would work with me on the cash flow issue as I was 75 percent of US sales. I also reasoned that we were partners building the market in the United States and that they would be lenient because they were breaching the contract by not getting product to me within the contracted timeframe. My assumptions were wrong, even a bit naive.

At the end of the day, success or failure depends primarily on the overall effectiveness of the entrepreneur. Topping the lists of reasons why entrepreneurs fail is lack of leadership, or the inability to see and respond to the business objectively. *New York Times* contributor Jay Goltz says it best: "One of the top reasons why businesses fail is owners who cannot get out of their own way. They may be stubborn, risk averse, conflict averse—meaning they need to be liked by *everyone* (even employees and vendors who can't do their jobs). They may be perfectionist, greedy, self-righteous, paranoid, indignant or insecure. You get the idea. Sometimes, you can even tell these owners the problem, and they will recognize that you are right—but continue to make the same mistakes over and over."[11]

Based on what we now know about mental models and automatic responses, we can certainly understand why. Even when entrepreneurs are aware that they might be the main problem, they are unable to change their behavior. Most entrepreneurs do not understand mental models or how routine thoughts and behaviors are formed. They have not yet learned that they can develop their ability to transform limiting or destructive mental models. They end up victims of their own thoughts and assumptions. They simply do not understand that they can choose to respond differently to the entrepreneurial process and the changing dynamics of their businesses.

COMMON MENTAL MODELS AND ENTREPRENEURS

Now that we have debunked the myths and helped you reframe your mental models about the entrepreneurial process, the next step is to reexamine the top five common mental models and highlight how they can play out for people thinking about starting—or already running—a business. Then we will look at new ways of thinking that can help shift these unproductive mental models for the entrepreneur.

INSECURITY: I AM NOT GOOD ENOUGH—I CANNOT ACCEPT MYSELF AS I AM, I AM LIMITED.

Let's start with this feeling of insecurity that many of us have. As we learned in Chapter 6, many of us tend to compensate for this nagging feeling of insecurity by constructing other mental models to disprove it. For many entrepreneurs, starting a business becomes the vehicle through which they try to communicate their value to the world. This is the first cognitive error: projecting too much meaning and value onto the venture. This is what I did. For many entrepreneurs, it is not about creating value for others, it is about *feeling* valuable. The first thing entrepreneurs must remember is that they are not their businesses. Going back to our logic about the subject-object relationship: everything that you are aware of or experience is an object of your awareness and therefore not you. Therefore, the entrepreneur is the Subject, and the business is the object. The entrepreneur is therefore not the business.

Based on our new understanding of the entrepreneurial process, we know that the entrepreneur is engaged in a process of creating and discovering the business. Every moment of the day, the entrepreneur is evaluating situations based on underlying assumptions, making decisions, and taking action. The challenge is that every decision and therefore every action is based on the entrepreneur's assumptions, which are based on everything the entrepreneur believes, including what they believe about themselves. If they are insecure and believe that they are not quite good enough, then it is possible that many of their decisions will be influenced by that assumption.

LESSON LEARNED

In my case, after leaving American Express, my business became my reason to feel good enough. Recall this Reality Check from Chapter 1: *Can you be objective and make good judgments when you are fearful? What was I afraid of at this point: losing my business, my reputation, or my self-concept?* Many of my subsequent decisions were influenced by my fear of losing my business, which was my reason to feel good. Therefore I was not objective.

In the next sections, we will take a closer look at the common mental models we often create in order to feel good enough: External Validation, Competition, Perfectionist, and Control.

EXTERNAL VALIDATION: I NEED OTHERS TO LIKE ME AND THINK I AM SMART.

One of the most debilitating mental models for an entrepreneur is the need for external validation. As we have seen, for many people, their self-worth is strongly tied to what others think. The 2012 US Global Entrepreneurship Monitor Report says, "Entrepreneurs and non-entrepreneurs are quite similar in their views that starting a business is a good career choice and that entrepreneurship leads to status."[12] This need for external validation can be so strong that entrepreneurs owe it to themselves to critically examine their motives. Starting a business or staying in a failing business because you need others to think that you made a good career choice, or that you will achieve some level of status as a result, can be quite destructive.

Entrepreneurs who need external validation rarely make good business decisions. Some entrepreneurs make the mistake of moving out of their home office too soon because they think it will show people they are successful. Others inflate their progress, their sales, their strategic alliances to others, often convincing themselves in the process that their inflated perceptions are true.

For many entrepreneurs, the business instantly becomes their identity. Have you noticed how much entrepreneurs talk about their businesses incessantly? This could either be a sign of passion or a sign of obsession. During a recent objectivity and entrepreneurship workshop, I was talking with an entrepreneur who said she was so identified with her business that when her friends invited her out to their normal hangouts, all she could talk about was her business. One day she found out that her friends had gotten together without her, and she was hurt. When she asked one of her friends about it, her friend told her, "All you talk about is your business, you are no fun anymore." But it is not just about being fun, or talking too much about your business, it is about whether you are able to be objective or make good decisions.

LESSON LEARNED

Recall this Reality Check: *Is it possible to be objective when you are totally defined by the job you have or the role you play?* Can you be objective about your business if your business becomes your identity and is the basis for you to receive external validation? The answer is no, it is not possible. This was my main cognitive error: magnifying the value of my business to be the basis for how I valued myself. I believe this is one of the reasons why I could not see things clearly and lost as much as I did. When I instantly became the Fruit Juice Lady, my identity and my self-worth became connected with my business. I could not separate it. When the business received its first container order, which was a lot of juice from a major distributor, I felt great about myself. And sometimes, when things didn't go as planned, I was concerned about how it would reflect on me and tried to justify it.

I often hear entrepreneurs say, "My business is my baby." I felt that way too. This really is the same thing. It is all about your identity. Most parents identify with being a parent, and many consider their children's behavior—performance or lack thereof—to be a reflection of themselves. Many will defend their children; they may overlook weaknesses, they may overinflate strengths, or they might put too much pressure on their children to succeed before they are ready. Does this sound familiar? Is it possible that thinking about your business as your baby reduces your ability to see things clearly and make sound judgments?

But passion *is* important. Loving what you do and having passion for your business are keys to success. So, how can you love what you do and have passion for your business without being identified or obsessed with it? How can you shift this unproductive mental model so that you can make better decisions?

NEW WAY OF THINKING

We have to start with our new data about the entrepreneurial process. As we have seen in the transformational learning process, knowledge and moments of insight based on new information are required for mental models to change. *You* have to decide that the mental model is no longer valid and is no longer serving you. We have also learned that successful entrepreneurs approach their ventures with a high degree of objectivity. They are means-driven, not goal-driven. They start with an assessment of who they are, what they know, or who they know. They know who they are, they value who they are, and are seeking to leverage their core gifts and strengths to explore a potential opportunity. They see their business concepts as ideas that may or may not be good business opportunities, but they have made the decision to pursue their idea up to a predetermined point. Successful entrepreneurs make an objective assessment up front regarding how much time, money, and personal commitment they want to invest in a business. They know that they have to take care of themselves and their families during the discovery phase of the business, and they have figured out how they are going to do that. They have rejected the mental model that passion means risking everything. The business is not defining them; they are defining how, and to what degree, their businesses fit into their lives. They know that they are not their businesses!

COMPETITION: I CONSTANTLY COMPARE MYSELF WITH OTHERS TO DETERMINE MY VALUE.

As we saw in Chapter 6, many of us are constantly comparing ourselves to others, and we often end up feeling bad about ourselves. This is just the way it has always been. We compare just about everything: grades, school admissions, offices, titles, cars, houses. So it is not surprising that entrepreneurs do the same thing. The competitive entrepreneur tends to set arbitrary benchmarks for success. In a recent workshop, an entrepreneur who was quite confident and competitive came up to me and said that he is concerned that after two years, he is only a million-dollar business when he is supposed to be a billion-dollar business. I asked him why he was putting that much pressure on himself. He then complained that other people in the workshop had higher revenues than him. I asked him why he was looking for a reason to feel bad about himself. Setting subjective goals for your business based on other's performance can blind you into making poor decisions or compel you to put even more illogical pressure on yourself. So why do it when there is, of course, an objective way of benchmarking? Look at industry profitability, solvency, and liquidity ratios to help you analyze your current financial condition. In fact, a Babson grad student and I created the Business Advantage Tool, a simple but comprehensive Excel workbook to help businesses do just that objective analysis.

PERFECTIONIST: I HAVE TO BE PERFECT IN EVERYTHING I DO.

This mental model is one of the reasons why many entrepreneurs remain solo and try to wear all the hats for much longer than is feasible. Many entrepreneurs cannot build a team, because this mental model impels them to do it all themselves in order for it to be right. They cannot tolerate it when things are not perfect. For some it can actually cause physical discomfort not to be involved in every aspect of their business. Clearly, this is not sustainable. Eventually, an entrepreneur crashes under the weight of it all and is forced to get help, sometimes too late.

As we have learned, the essence of the entrepreneurial process is taking action, learning, and acting again. Another problem with the Perfectionist mental model is that it's paralyzing. These folks tend to overanalyze and are not comfortable proceeding without perfect information. We now know that there is no such thing as perfect information, and that the key to success is acting based on the available information and being comfortable with pivoting based on the results of those actions. Successful entrepreneurs have not only learned how to pivot, but they also have learned to value an opportunity to pivot. To them, it means they have learned something new about their business model: the customer, the competition, or strategic partners that has presented an even better opportunity than was originally contemplated. Hooray. Whereas the perfectionist entrepreneur interprets pivoting to mean that the analysis was wrong, and the focus is on getting things back on track.

NEW WAY OF THINKING

Given that the world is largely unpredictable, uncontrollable, and unknowable, can any of us afford to be perfectionists when the result will inevitably be failure? While some corporate leaders may feel more certain and operate with the illusion of control, predictability, and knowability, entrepreneurs must understand, embrace, and thrive in the reality that entrepreneurship is not certain and perfection is not the goal.

CONTROL: I MUST BE ABLE TO CONTROL MY ENVIRONMENT. MY SELF-CONCEPT IS BASED ON HOW WELL I CAN CONTROL PEOPLE AND OUTCOMES.

As demonstrated in Chapter 6, the Perfectionist and Control mental models often go hand in hand. Many entrepreneurs make the assumption that if they do everything perfectly then they will be able to control outcomes. This is a mistake. I am sure we can all think of situations where we did everything that was within our power to do, and we did it perfectly, yet we did not achieve the desired results.

NEW WAYS OF THINKING

As we discussed in Chapter 6, one of the four fundamental principles of objectivity is "We cannot always control the results of our actions." While we can know that the actions and motivations of others can impact our results, which can be considered known variables, we often don't know to what degree. Then there are all the unknown variables, things we can't anticipate at all, that can change the results of our actions. Entrepreneurs must give up their need to control external factors and learn how to respond objectively to the unexpected. Now that we know that the entrepreneurial process is more of an objective discovery process, entrepreneurs can begin the process of shifting from the mental model of control to a mental model of expecting and embracing the unexpected. Instead of feeling disappointed when things outside of their control impact their results, entrepreneurs must think about what they have learned and determine the next best action. Make lemonade out of lemons! Successful entrepreneurs' only interest in control is becoming self-aware enough to control the one thing they can control: themselves, and their responses to the uncontrollable. They focus on questioning and evaluating their underlying assumptions before taking action. They become acutely aware of their triggers so that they reduce their tendency to over-react to unexpected situations while they are in the process of shifting this unproductive and limiting mental model.

AN ENTREPRENEUR'S TRANSFORMATION

Clearly the entrepreneurship process is centered on the entrepreneur. How that entrepreneur feels about himself, the entrepreneurial process, and the world is the guiding influence for every thought and action. I recently coached a lovely and very competent woman, married and in her mid-30s, who had just left her full-time job to take on consulting work to have more flexibility and to focus on starting her own business. She was frustrated because she absolutely knew that she was getting in her own way, and she wanted to stop. She had taken one of my classes and learned the basics but didn't remember how to start the process of shifting unproductive mental models. In her own words, she describes how she is working on transforming her mental models:

> I'm an independent person who always liked to question author-
> ity and make my own path. I sought out difficult challenges and
> liked to overcome them. A classic overachiever, I tried to be perfect.
> Academically, I graduated at the top of my class in college and went

on to graduate school at Yale. Starting in my 20s, I did a lot of different things in my career, from teaching to data analytics to sales. It has always been my dream to be an entrepreneur. Throughout my career, this dream was in the back of my mind. Most days I thought about it and felt a distinct sadness when I thought about building a career and climbing the corporate ladder. I always seemed to wind up with bad bosses who did not support my successes. Instead, I felt they were intimidated by me and worked to keep me under their thumb. After finishing up my MBA from Babson College and being laid off from a pharmaceutical company, I decided the time was right. I had the idea, the right background, the right technology, and a network of pertinent colleagues I could tap.

As I started the journey, I began to realize that I was getting in my own way. I found successes that should have built my confidence. I validated the concept with potential clients, and there was clearly a market need. I joined the Microsoft BizSpark program, a start-up incubator for technology companies. I built critical relationships necessary for going to market with strategic partners. But I came to realize that my self-doubts were invading my thoughts and throwing me off my game. I could normally muster up enough strength to make it through that critical meeting or presentation, but a constant feeling of self-doubt permeated my thinking, always there to beat me up at a moment's notice.

A popular thought of mine was that no one will take me seriously once they meet me in person. I only do well over the phone. *There is something about my appearance and countenance that inspires a lack of confidence*, I thought. When bumps in the road occurred (as they always do for entrepreneurs), I found myself saying, *See that, you don't have what it takes. Who are you kidding? You'll never be able to do this.* My rational mind told me this was foolishness, but the thoughts wouldn't go away. I knew I had to change to succeed. If I didn't, I'd be working for someone else the rest of my life.

That's when I started to think seriously about the concept of objectivity that I remembered from a class I had taken at Babson. Somehow I knew that was the answer. From the outside looking in, I had everything a rational person could possibly need to succeed. I reached out to Elizabeth Thornton to have lunch. That is where my transformation began.

The idea that I had mental models that were no longer serving me (but actually working against me) hit me hard. I was so determined to stop it—I am still working on it as I write today. I wanted to snap my fingers and change the negative self-talk. I knew it would not be that easy. I had to do the work of figuring out (1) what are my mental models and where did they originate; (2) what mental models do I want to have moving forward; and (3) how would I make the transformation and unlock the door to my future? I am somewhere between steps 2 and 3 today. Looking back on my life, I slowly began to realize that I had created and was still operating under several mental models, including:

- **No talents**. I am not inherently good at anything; my successes have occurred only due to hard work.
- **Expect difficulties**. Life is really hard and you have to muscle through everything. People are trying to see to it that you do not succeed.
- **Authority is bad**. Authority figures are always incompetent and have bad intentions.

Looking back, I realize where these models took shape. Childhood was not easy for me. I grew up in a home where I was told I did not have any real talents or abilities, but since I worked hard, I was able to overcome these deficiencies. Life was always hard and to get ahead you had to prepare and work harder than anyone else. Mental abuse from my father was common, so I learned early on to distrust authority. How was this playing out in my adult life? I was sabotaging relationships with people in authority, such as bosses. This reinforced my theory that authority is inherently bad and life will always be difficult. Because of my "No talent" mental model, I was consistently overlooking and heavily discounting any talents I had, believing that any success I had was due to thorough preparation. This left me with little to no self-confidence, always feeling like I was never prepared enough. To be an entrepreneur, you have to be confident. If you don't believe in yourself, no one else will. Here is where I was hitting a major road block to my success. How was I going to have an organization that people could believe in if the founder was fabricating crazy ideas in her head? It had to stop now. It was time to shed the cocoon and fly.

When I started making the links between these models and my behavior, I felt pretty liberated. But the feelings of self-doubt were still there. I realized that I had to do the work of "undoing" the old mental models and creating new ones. How would I do that? First I needed to write down what I truly believed about myself, objectively; i.e., what are my new mental models?

- I am a creative, conscientious person with many individual talents that will make me successful.
- If you accomplish something, it does not have to be difficult or hard. Be optimistic. They will take you seriously.
- Authority is necessary and not always bad (or good).

I decided that in order to believe these models, I had to live them. In order to live them, I had to believe them. Which one comes first? I decided I would start by reminding myself of these truths by posting sticky notes...everywhere. "I am unique," "I am intelligent," "I am compassionate," and other affirmations were posted in my bathroom, in the kitchen, on my desk, in my car. Any place I spent time alone I posted these notes to remind myself of what I really believed. It was my response to the negative self-talk that was haunting me.

I kept a journal (which I typically do not do) that became an important outlet to reinforce a new way of thinking. I wrote down successes, failures, frustrations. There were days when I knew I had fallen back into my old patterns, so I wrote down what happened and analyzed it. It happened quite a lot, given that I was in a sales job at the time. I was faced with rejection most every day, a ripe environment for personal development! My boss once told me that I had to present myself more strategically in our monthly business development meetings, because I wasn't getting value across that I was bringing to the organization. The old me jumped all over that one. I immediately jumped to the conclusion that people don't take me seriously because of some intrinsic quality I have (or don't have).

I felt pretty bad that day. When I jotted down the story, it became crystal clear that I was creating inferences that were based on old mental models. There could be a thousand other reasons why my boss would say this—I was new at sales, to the organization, and just needed to learn the ropes. Perhaps he was trying to convince me to assert myself more because he believed in me. I wrote these down. What became clear is that there was no clear explanation. At the end of the day, it comes down to how I choose to think about it. I had control; it did not have control over me. Over time, I became better at heading off the altercation with the old me before she could do any damage.

One example happened when I walked into the bank one afternoon to open an account for my new business venture. I was shuttled over to meet with a VP who looked just like the kind of guy who was going to judge me based on my appearance. In my language, that meant he would think I was a moron because of the way I looked. As I stood there waiting for him to finish up his phone call, I thought about it. *I can choose to think he is going to prejudge me based on my appearance, or I can believe he will not.* I thought of my sticky note that said "I am unique." What makes me different makes me a more interesting person. *He's going to like me and believe in what I am doing.* I took a different mindset and saw myself for what I had rather than what I did not have.

When I sat down, I looked him straight in the eye and smiled warmly. It was a great meeting, and I walked out with a lot more than just a checking account. He introduced me to the branch manager and said they were interested in helping me any way possible as I grow my business. He called me a few days later and showed sincere interest in helping finance the venture when the time was right. This is what it felt like to be comfortable in my own skin, and it felt good, I thought.

Slowly but surely, this work started to change my thinking, my behavior, and my life. I lost 15 pounds. I realized I would always stress about not being prepared enough and would eat my way to comfort. That started to change, as I was no longer eating to dull the nervousness. I felt a sense of peace overtake my being, as I started to accept myself, not as I thought I was, but as I actually am in reality. Though I am still on my journey, I feel I am finally on the right path. Somehow realizing my dream as an entrepreneur, I believe, will help me evolve into the person I was meant to be: confident, compassionate, optimistic, and secure.

You might be reading this and wonder, How do I get started? I tell you the first step is to want something different, really want something different badly. Why? Because it takes motivation, drive, and energy to change old ways of operating. I liken it to exercising more. The results you see drive you to do it every day, and it gets easier as you go. But you have to want the benefits more than you want the old ways of living. Otherwise, you can't sustain it. But unlike exercise, I find that the work I do pays dividends toward the future. What I mean by that is, if I stop exercising for six months, I will probably lose most of the benefits. I didn't see that during this transformation. It is more like riding a bike in that regard—you don't forget how to do it once you figure it out. Yes, you will fall off the bike sometimes, but as long as you get back on, you will get to where you are headed. And it definitely beats the old way. It becomes a no-brainer, and people will notice the difference. You have to do the work to figure out your mental models, and then you have to validate what you believe with someone you trust who knows you well. Let's face it: we may think we know ourselves, but we may be focusing too much or not focusing enough on certain areas. The next step is to make it real by practicing a new way of operating. You have to figure out what it will take to get that red flag to pop up in your head when you are operating against mental models that do not serve you. Once you see the flag, you can intervene. Plan your interventions ahead of time and closely analyze situations when you think you missed the boat. Next time you will be better.

I hope you can relate to what this person is saying. Frankly, I am very happy for her because, within a very short period of time, she was able to shift her mental models to a point where she was no longer a victim of her mind, limited by her own thoughts. She is a perfect example of the power of attention density, the singular focus that is essential in transforming unproductive and destructive mental models. I hope her story has inspired you. In the next chapter I will give you specific tools so that if or when you decide to go out on your own and start your own venture, you will be armed with an objective approach to building a sustainable business model.

Chapter 10

THE OBJECTIVE ENTREPRENEUR'S BUSINESS MODEL MAP

Now that you understand the entrepreneurial process and how entrepreneurs really think and act, and if you are seriously considering it, the next step is to empower yourself with the tools to help you get started. There are several highly effective tools, methodologies, and frameworks on the market today to help entrepreneurs start and grow sustainable businesses. If you are already an entrepreneur, you may have already seen the Alexander Osterwalder and Yves Pigneur Business Model Canvas, Eric Ries's Lean Startup methodology, or perhaps Steve Blank's Lean Launch Pad. While each has its own unique value, all are grounded in the new thinking that the entrepreneurial process is a journey of objective discovery. Here is a brief overview of each.

Specifically, in Ries's book *The Lean Startup: How Today's Entrepreneurs Use Continuous Innovation to Create Radically Successful Businesses*, he explains that the "Lean Startup method is designed to teach you how to start a business. Instead of making complex plans that are based on a lot of assumptions, you can make constant adjustments with a steering wheel called the Build-Measure-Learn feedback loop. Through this process of steering, you can learn when and if it's time to make a sharp turn called a pivot or whether we should persevere along the current path."

A core component of Ries's methodology is the minimum viable product (MVP). The MVP is the product with just the necessary features to get money and feedback from early adopters. He suggests that the first step is identifying a problem that needs to be solved and then developing an MVP to begin the process of learning as quickly as possible. Once the MVP is established, a start-up can work on shaping the opportunity. When this process of measuring and learning is done correctly, it will be clear that a company is either discovering a sustainable business model or not. "If not, it is a sign that it is time to pivot or make a structural course correction to test a new fundamental hypothesis about the product, strategy, and engine of growth. Once your engine is revved up, the Lean Startup offers methods to scale and grow businesses, with maximum acceleration."[1]

Alexander Osterwalder and Yves Pigneur's Business Model Canvas is the tool we use at Babson to help guide students through the entrepreneurial process. Osterwalder and Pigneur describe the canvas this way: "It allows an entrepreneur to describe, design, challenge, invent, and pivot the nine building blocks of a business model. It is based on the definition that a business model describes the rationale of how an organization creates, delivers, and captures value."[2]

And finally, the Lean Launch Pad, leveraging Osterwalder's and Pigneur's work, is based on the assertion that startups are *not* smaller versions of large companies with known business models that primarily follow a predictive approach to problem solving and decision making. Steve Blank and his Lean Launch Pad team think of start-ups as temporary organizations in search of an unknown business model. This temporary organization is designed to search for a repeatable and scalable business model through a process of testing hypotheses, gathering early and frequent customer feedback, and showing MVPs to prospects. The Lean Launch Pad teaches entrepreneurs that launching a business is a search process (of customer discovery and validation) and an execution process (of customer creation and company building).[3]

Complementing the pioneering work of Osterwalder and Pigneur, Ries, Blank, and my colleagues at Babson College, the Objective Entrepreneur's Business Model Map is based on the premise that new venture creation is not separate from the entrepreneur and that an entrepreneur's ability to be objective ultimately determines success or failure. Unproductive mental models often impede an entrepreneur's ability to test a hypothesis, respond objectively to customer feedback, and identify when to pivot. The goal of the Objective Entrepreneur's Business Model Map is to highlight the key components of the business model discovery process and provide tips and new ways of thinking to ensure that you are engaging the entrepreneurial process with greater objectivity.

The Objective Entrepreneur's Business Model Map covers the four main areas of business model development: Value Proposition and Customer Segments, Channels and Customer Experience, Infrastructure and Resources, and Financial Viability and Access to Capital.

The key to this map:

1. Entrepreneurship is a process of objective discovery.
2. To be an objective entrepreneur means knowing that you are the Subject. You are not your business.
3. Framework for the objective entrepreneur:
   a. Identify assumptions, preferences, and expectations first.
   b. Nonjudgmentally formulate the hypotheses to be tested.
   c. Design an objective process for testing hypotheses through direct customer engagement.
   d. Learn from results of action without projecting long-term impact.
   e. Take next action without specific preconceived expectations.

The Objective Entrepreneur's Business Model Map

Component #1 Unique Value Proposition (UVP) and Customers	Component #2 Channels and Customer Experience	Component #3 Infrastructure and Resources	Component #4 Financial Viability—Financial Requirements

Problem Identification
• What is the problem?
• What is the annoyance?
• What is the unmet need?
• Who has the problem?
 	
Core Value Proposition (CVP)
What is the core benefit?
 	
Customers:
List all potential customers who could benefit from the CVP?
List UVP for all potential customers?
 	
Minimum Viable Product (MVP)
Whenever possible create a product or rendering for each customer segment to validate assumptions about Customers and UVP
	Channels
	For each Customer/UVP, ask:
	• How do my customers want to engage and buy products?
	• Through what channels, online, wholesale, retail...?
	• Should they be owned or partner channels?
	• Who are potential partner channels?
	• How will they help engage my customers?
	
	Customer Experience
	For each Customer/UVP, ask:
	• How do my customers want to learn about my products/ services?
	• How do my customers want to interact with me through purchase, delivery, and after purchase?
		Infrastructure Activities
		• What are the primary activities, that directly generate a product or service, such as sourcing product inputs, manufacturing, delivery?
		• What are the secondary activities related to the sales and support of the product and service such as channel development, brand management, customer relationship management?
		• What are the key business operational activites; such as legal, financial management, office management?
		
		Resource Requirements
		• What are the human resource needs to establish and maintain infrastructure?
			• Pricing—What are my channels and customers' willingness to pay
			• Profitability—How will I generate revenue through the channels?
			  • What are my costs for producing my products?
			  • What is my gross margin?
			• Start-up Costs: What are my costs to set up operations?
			• Operating Expenses and Working Capital–What are my fixed operating costs for office, people, etc.?
			• What are my brand development costs?
			• What is my profit margin?
			• What is my burn rate?
			• How much money do I need to raise?

Keys to Map	To be an objective entrepreneur means knowing that you are the Subject. You are not your business.	Entrepreneurship is a process of objective discovery	✓ Identify assumptions, preferences, and expectations first! ✓ Non-judgmentally formulate the hypotheses to be tested ✓ Design an objective process for testing hypotheses ✓ Learn from results of action without projecting long term impact ✓ Take next action without specific preconceived expectations

VALUE PROPOSITION AND CUSTOMER SEGMENTS

Most entrepreneurs begin the entrepreneurial process with a problem that they are seeking to solve. From their own experiences or the experiences of others, they have identified a real need that has not been met, an inconvenience that no longer needs to be tolerated, or a real problem that needs to be solved. This is the value proposition: the value or benefit your product or services will deliver to solve a problem or fulfill a need for a customer. At the point of problem recognition or identification, the entrepreneur can also envision a customer. Often it is difficult for the entrepreneur to separate the two. The customer is the specific group of people or organizations that have the need that you are trying to satisfy, the pain point you are seeking to relieve, the problem you are trying to solve. Of course, when the problem and the customer first occur in the entrepreneur's mind, it is not a comprehensive list of all the potential customers or customer segments. Entrepreneurs must then go beyond that initial assumption about who the customer is, validate a hypothesis that a real problem exists for a particular group of customers, and then explore all other possible customer segments.

The problem is that many times entrepreneurs make assumptions about what people need or would pay for without actually talking to potential customers. They end up building the perfect solution for a problem that may not really exist. Another problem that I have seen is when an entrepreneur identifies and validates a solution for a particular customer segment and ignores all other possible customer segments. For example, I was working with an inventor who observed, during one of his camping trips with his family, that mothers had a very difficult time spraying mosquito repellent on their children. The wind would gust, and invariably the spray would end up everywhere except on the child. He went back home and invented the Mosquito Mitt, a unique glove that would allow the mother to spray mosquito repellent directly onto the glove and then apply it evenly on the skin of the child. When he identified the problem, he assumed that the target market was mothers with children who engage in outdoor activities. While this was clearly one customer segment, there were many more. It turned out that many different types of people loved the product. Some people preferred to use it as a furniture-polishing glove, and therefore he needed to explore the household accessory market. Others preferred to use it as a glove to wax their cars, which meant that it could also be an after-market automobile accessory. Then he found that owners of horses had an even greater pain point because it was very difficult to safely apply fly sprays and other grooming products to horses. Hence it could also be an equestrian grooming accessory.

What is the lesson here? There are many products on the market today that are used by different customer segments to deliver varying value propositions. The objective entrepreneur must step back and resist the natural tendency to label things, put things in boxes, and create mental models that can limit new ways of thinking. When an entrepreneur identifies a specific problem and thinks of a solution (for instance, the difficulty of safely applying mosquito repellent), the entrepreneur must stop and ask himself what is the core value proposition, or CVP. The CVP is the fundamental benefit that your product provides. In this case it was the ability to safely and cleanly apply any liquid substance to any surface, human or otherwise. Once the entrepreneur identifies the CVP, the entrepreneur can then brainstorm about all the possible customer segments that could benefit from this CVP. Had he done so, this ingenious entrepreneur might not have initially branded his first product the Mosquito Mitt when it was far more than that.

Once the CVP is clearly defined, then the next step is to develop an MVP. Steve Blank describes it this way: "The MVP is a 'low-fidelity' product that can be as simple as a landing page with your value proposition, benefits summary, and a call to action to learn more, answer a short survey, or preorder. It could even be a quick website prototype built in PowerPoint or with a simple landing-page creation tool. Your goal is something basic—no fancy U/I [user interface], logos, or animation."[4]

The next step is to put the MVP to the test by engaging with as many customers as possible. If you are using a website as your MVP, you can certainly measure conversion rates to determine response. But be sure to determine the conversion rate that signifies a positive response in your specific case—is it 20 percent? Is it 50 percent? To add more objectivity to the process, experts suggest you conduct as many in-person interviews with as many customers and customer segments you can. Using the same MVP, sit down with customers and see their responses firsthand, and have a list of open-ended questions to ask that will help you learn more about your customers and their needs. I recommend that you talk to a minimum of 20 people for every assumption you are trying to validate, which means you could end up conducting far more than 100 interviews. Your goal is to learn, without preconceived notions or expectations.

To discover the Value Proposition and Customer Segments component of the business model, entrepreneurs must design a hypotheses testing process that is objective. Here are some tips.

First, to create your interview list of your first 20 potential customers, start with your most likely potential customers and/or customer segments for the CVP and ask yourself if you have a preference for or bias toward targeting a certain group. It is possible that you may have assumptions that one segment may be easier to reach, may have a greater potential to provide reviews and customer feedback, or have the greatest potential for repeat sales. Understanding your assumptions and preferences prior to beginning the interview process will help you be more objective. You must also be aware of our natural tendency to want our assumptions, hypotheses, and ideas to be validated. Most of us really do like to be right, and we will go a long way to avoid admitting we were wrong. Because we know now how our expectations can influence our interpretations of our perceptions, it is possible that we will only hear what we want to hear. For example, you might still hear and record an interview response of "Yeah, I guess I will pay $50 for that" as a firm "Yes, I would pay $50 for that and I will refer it to others." If you find yourself too concerned about the outcome of the interviews and you are unable to approach the interviews as a discovery process, it might also be a good idea to have others, who are less invested in the process, conduct the interviews.

Second, create a list of your *least likely* customers and customer segments that you assume will either not get it, not be able to use it, not like it, et cetera. Use the objectivity-in-the-moment technique and do the opposite of what your mind is telling you. If you are thinking about targeting millennials, interview ten baby boomers as well, just to be sure.

Third, ask the questions in a way in which it is easier for the person to say no rather than yes. That way, if they respond affirmatively, it is more of an active, versus passive, response. Again, whenever possible, ask open-ended questions so you get a deeper sense of the customer's problem or pain point.

The output from your Value Proposition and Customer Segments component of the business model could reveal more customer segments than you originally imagined, as was the case with the Mosquito Mitt. The next step is to assess how many potential customers exist for each of your segments. It is at this stage, when the UVP, CVP, and customer segments have been identified and validated, that market research is useful. An objective entrepreneur will conduct an industry and market analysis to begin to quantify the opportunity. For many, understanding market demand, the industry, and the competitive landscape is daunting, but successful entrepreneurs always know their business. Entrepreneurs often think they have no competition, that there is nothing out there like their product or service. This is never the case. To be objective, an entrepreneur must understand that there is always some form of competition. It could be rivalry from a direct competitor or just inertia, people doing it one way and being resistant to change. The entrepreneur must conduct an in-depth industry analysis to understand how the industry is operating so that he or she can determine how to effectively compete for market share. Here is a list of some, but not all, of the questions the entrepreneur must be able to answer:

- How large is the overall market, and what is the potential for capturing market share?
- What is the size of the market segments I have identified?
- How many potential customers can I realistically reach?
- Is it an emerging industry or is the industry declining?
- What is the year-over-year growth rate in the industry?
- What trends are influencing the industry, and what do they portend?
- Is the industry concentrated with a few players holding a large percentage of market share, or is the industry fragmented with a lot of companies each holding a small percentage of market share?
- What are the substitute products?
- What is the nature of the competition between the existing players in the industry? Is the rivalry intense?
- Is there significant variability in profitability within the industry?
- On what basis do the competitors compete? Is it based on price, customer service, convenience, or other factors?
- What are the competitive strategies of the leading firms in the industry?
- Are there proprietary barriers to entry in the industry?

It is relatively easy to be objective about analyzing the economic and strategic characteristics of an entire industry. The facts are more clearly laid out. It is the subjective interpretation of these facts where entrepreneurs can get into trouble. For example, if the industry is growing by 10 percent year over year, an entrepreneur cannot assume that it will continue to grow at that rate. Moreover, if the 10 percent growth is the industry average, the entrepreneur must determine if there are companies within the industry that are growing above or below that industry average and what may account for the variability. The entrepreneur must continually dig deeper to understand what trends are driving the growth rate. The entrepreneur must make an objective assessment as to whether the trends may continue or what could cause a shift in that trend. While making this assessment, the entrepreneur realizes that he or she has limited knowledge and that the assessment could be wrong. Interpreting data and forecasting trends in an effort to reduce uncertainty is an entrepreneurial activity that requires the most objectivity. Typically, when faced with making this type of assessment, the entrepreneur goes one of two ways. Some entrepreneurs, because of background and life experience, will be pessimistic and see the glass as half empty. The pessimist often thinks the absolute worst and plans accordingly. On the other hand, an optimist who always sees the glass half full will plan for the best-case scenario. Which of these entrepreneurs is most likely correct? Is either one being objective?

Objectivity means looking at the glass without the judgment of full or empty. Rather than the optimistic or pessimistic views, to be objective means looking at the market conditions as neither good nor bad, but just as they are. By looking at the market conditions and their potential impact without labeling them good or bad, an entrepreneur can approach the marketplace more effectively. Knowing that there is imperfect information, the objective entrepreneur analyzes the potential variables and develops a risk assessment for each, then takes the next best action.

CHANNELS AND CUSTOMER EXPERIENCE

The next step is to discover the most effective way to reach, communicate with, and build a relationship with your customer segments. Specifically, the entrepreneur must determine how to raise awareness and engage the customer with products and services. The entrepreneur must discover the most user-friendly and efficient process for customers to buy the product and how best to deliver the product to the customer. Lastly, the entrepreneur must learn from potential customers how to provide ongoing support and maintain a relationship with that customer.

The first consideration is whether to create or use your own existing channels to reach your customers or whether to use partner channels. Owned channels would be direct to the customers through brick-and-mortar establishments, through your own sales force or website. Indirect channels include wholesale distribution, retail, or through partner's sales organization and websites. While owned channels can have higher margins than partner channels, it takes more time and money to establish owned channels.

To approach these building blocks objectively, entrepreneurs must first look at this question in terms of the customer only. Sadly, some entrepreneurs make this decision based purely on their own preferences, or driven by their egos. Some entrepreneurs believe showing people that they have built their own distribution channels—their own storefronts, sales forces, or online presence—is a sign of success. It is an ego boost, to be sure. But be acutely aware that mental models about external validation, and cognitive distortions equating your business success with your own value, are often at work—however subtly—in these types of decisions. While you are in the process of transforming these, ground yourself in the new data about trends underlying consumer buying behavior. Remember, it is with new knowledge and information that you can challenge your underlying assumptions and mental models. Are you keeping up with the latest trends in consumer purchasing behavior, which will, after all, have far more impact on how your product performs than whether the website bears your name?

This is the age of the "hyper-aware consumer." According to *Entrepreneur Magazine*'s Dan Newman, "Buyers are between 70 and 90 percent of the way through a sales process before they even engage a company."[5] They have already compared your product with everything else on the market; they have elicited the buying experience of others who have purchased the product; and they know exactly what they want and how much they should pay for it. Think about it, have you bought anything truly meaningful lately without doing a little research first? What does this mean for your customer acquisition strategy?

And then there is the proliferation of online sales. Entrepreneurs cannot assume which products are best sold online and which are best sold in stores. It could be both. Depending on the product category, some online customers are satisfied with buying experiences that begin and end with the online store. They really don't want human involvement at all. Others prefer to do their research online and then go to the store to make the purchase. While it may appear that online sales continue to be mostly for small-ticket items, some homes, cars, and high-end technology products are bought online as well. What are your assumptions? Some entrepreneurs maintain that even in this era of one-click shopping, figuring out a way to make a person feel special and valued is the key to building and maintaining customer relationships.

I was recently leading a workshop in New York with fashion entrepreneurs. We were talking about distribution channels and social media strategies to drive awareness and sales. Samantha, a very talented jewelry entrepreneur, shared that instead of investing in creating her own e-commerce website and showroom, she decided to partner with a leading marketing partner who provided the website, the showroom, and public relations exposure in top magazines and newspapers. This was a bundled service that she could afford. She was objective and did not care about owning her own website. Then, for the next year, she focused on building her brand through social media. In just one year she had 19,000 Facebook friends and 12,000 Instagram followers. She said whenever she posted a picture of a new item in Instagram and then linked it to Facebook, she could immediately see the uptick in sales on her partner's website. Because she was able to establish strong, measurable awareness and buying relationships with her target customers, her brand got the attention of major retailers. In fact, she landed a spot on the Home Shopping Network for fall 2014. It all comes down to understanding your target customers—how they want to interact with you and how they want to buy.

Unfortunately, many entrepreneurs underestimate the foundational importance of sales channels and customer relationships. Many still have a mental model that says, "If I build it, they will come." To be objective requires that you talk to more potential customers. But before you do, uncover any hidden mental models or preferences you may have. Here are some tips:

1. Start with your preferences, what *you* want to do.

    a. How do I prefer to reach the customer?

    b. How do I prefer to sell to my customers?

2. Then think about your assumptions about how they want to be reached and how your customers want to purchase.

    a. This step is critical. If you notice a tendency to make assumptions based on what you prefer, then you can be more objective when talking to customers. Remember, bringing your mental models to conscious awareness is the first step in being objective.

3. Instead of relying on your initial assumptions and preferences, create a list of all your possible channels for each of your customer segments. You cannot assume that all customer segments want to engage with you in the same way.

    a. Investigate where and how your targeted customers buy similar products or services. Going back to our example of the Mosquito Mitt, if one of the market segments is women who shop for household items, ask yourself how women find out about new products on the market. Where and how do people shop for household items? Do they go to supermarkets, drug stores, Walmart, Target? Or do they buy these items online, or both? If your customer segment is horse owners and trainers, how do they learn of new products for horses? Where and how do they buy grooming products for their horses? Clearly, the same product targeted to a different customer segment will not be found or purchased in the same way. What type of relationship do these customers have with vendors of similar products they purchase? What kind of relationship do they prefer to have with you? Do they use social media? Do they use comparison websites before they purchase? You get the idea.

4. Once you have identified all of your hypotheses, test them. At this stage I recommend at least ten customer interviews for each customer segment.

Once you have discovered the optimal distribution channels and customer relationships for each customer segment, you can begin to develop your marketing and branding strategies, which may include content marketing, such as blogging and videos, and social media campaigns to build customer referrals. You will also be able to forecast customer acquisition and retention costs and start to identify your highest-value customers and channels.

INFRASTRUCTURE AND RESOURCES

By this time in the process, most entrepreneurs feel pretty good. They have discovered a solution to an unmet need of a clearly defined customer, and they understand the best way to motivate, engage, and support these customers. This is a major accomplishment. Many entrepreneurs will find that many of their hypotheses along the way did not stand the test of objective inquiry, and they had to go in a different direction. They embraced the pivot and pivoted successfully, finding either a revised solution or a different customer or perhaps even a stronger, more compelling value proposition. Now that this significant milestone has been reached, the next step is to determine the resources and infrastructure you will need to deliver that value to the targeted customer.

The focus is now on identifying and acquiring the required resources and setting up initial operations. The goal of the entrepreneur is to establish an infrastructure that will allow the company to deliver value to the identified and validated customer segments. The entrepreneur should focus on defining the value chain, the specific activities that are required to motivate the customers' willingness to pay for the company's product or service. The first step is identifying the primary activities, those that directly generate a product or service. These are the physical resources such as manufacturing facilities, equipment, buildings, and vehicles that are needed to create value. The entrepreneur must evaluate whether these resources should be acquired or purchased outright or outsourced. Most entrepreneurs outsource key manufacturing functions for their businesses but make the mistake of only establishing a single source. For example, a start-up entrepreneur with a men's skin-care line with unique natural inputs only found one resource for a key ingredient in one of his top-selling products. When his one resource ran out of this key input, he had no choice but to put those new customers' orders on back order until he could strengthen the supply chain with other sources. A good rule of thumb for entrepreneurs in the process of setting up their physical infrastructure is to outsource versus internally develop, lease versus buy, and try to negotiate favorable payment terms to minimize cash outlays up front.

Once the entrepreneur has determined how to create the product, the next step is to consider the infrastructure or systems requirements to facilitate the sale and support of the product. This will include the key activities that were identified in the Channels and Customer Experience component of the business model. These include channel development; retail, wholesale, owned or partner websites, and brand management; content development, content management, social media platforms; et cetera.

The next infrastructure resource decision involves human resources, the team that is needed to deliver the value to the customer. This is also a key part of the business model. As we reviewed earlier, this is an area where some entrepreneurs struggle with subjectivity. As we have seen, many entrepreneurs have mental models that impel them to do everything on their own, and often they believe they have skills that they really don't have.

To approach the Infrastructure and Resources component of the business model with more objectivity, it is helpful to use a simple infrastructure and resources requirement grid: In step 1, the entrepreneur will identify the critical activities required. In step 2, the entrepreneur will determine if the activity should be performed in-house or outsourced to strategic partners. In steps 3 and 4, the entrepreneur must determine if he or she has the skills required to perform or manage the activity and if there is a gap that needs to be filled. In step 5, the entrepreneur determines whether to hire an employee or engage a contractor to fill the gap. For example, the model on the next page represents the preliminary thinking of a CEO of an emerging dress designer.

Infrastructure and Resources Requirement Grid

Step 1	Step 2	Step 3	Step 4	Step 5
ACTIVITIES	In-house or outsource?	Skills needed to perform or manage?	Do I have the time or the skills? Is there a gap?	Hire in or contract out?
Supply Chain Management:				
Sourcing product inputs	In-house	5–7 years operations or supply chain management	Some, gap	Key activity of CEO initially, then hire
Manufacturing	Outsource			
Product delivery	Outsource			
Brand Management:				
Content development, blogs, videos	In-house	3–5 years experience in brand management	No, gap	Hire
Content management, social media platforms	In-house	3–5 years business development	No, gap	Hire
Channel Development:				
Channel acquisition: retailers, wholesales, websites	In-house	5–7 years business development	Yes, no gap	Key activity of the CEO
Managing channel relationships	In-house	5–7 years partner development and relationship management	Yes, no gap	Key activity of the CEO

Day to Day Operations:				
Office management	In-house	3–5 years office management for small business	No, gap	Hire one person for both activities
Customer relationship management, inquiries, complaints	In-house	3–5 years customer service experience	No, gap	Hire one person for both activities
Financial Management:				
Establishing processes to collect financial data, financial statement development Managing payables and receivables	Outsource	5–10 years working with start-up businesses in industry	No, gap	Contract out
Financial statement analysis and ongoing monitoring of financial health of the company	In-house	5–10 years working with start-ups and early stage businesses	No, gap	Hire Key activity of the CEO
Legal:				
Review partnership and outsource contracts Develop employment contracts	Outsource	5–10 years working with start-up businesses	No, gap	Contract out

FINANCIAL VIABILITY AND ACCESS TO CAPITAL

Now that the entrepreneur clearly understands what resources will be needed to develop the infrastructure of his organization, the next step is to focus on the economics of the business to determine the financial viability of the venture. This is another area where objectivity is tough but essential. I have seen countless entrepreneurs start a business without knowing if the business will be profitable. Many have a mental model that if they sell enough, eventually the business will make money. This is not just blinding optimism. Frankly, many people, if they have not gone to business school, may not know how to correctly approach the analysis. I have worked with many entrepreneurs who have been in business for two or three years and they do not know their gross margin, or even the meaning of the metric. This is not uncommon. The problem is that many of us with Perfectionist, Competition, or External Validation mental models have a tendency to avoid the things we are not naturally good at or that we don't understand. Entrepreneurs must overcome this subjective tendency. Understanding financial management is not something that can be avoided, nor is the lack of understanding of financial statements something to be ashamed of. The reality is that there are many creative people, without financial acumen, who can actually design innovative solutions to problems. And conversely, many financial analyst types don't have a creative bone in their body. But given that this is so important, the entrepreneur must engage a key member of the team to routinely conduct this analysis and help the entrepreneur understand how the business makes money even if they can't do spreadsheets. Many entrepreneurs may outsource the data entry to a bookkeeper, who will set up QuickBooks or an equivalent to input financial transactions. Once that is done, however, the entrepreneur should eventually learn what the data means.

Broadly speaking, the entrepreneur must understand whether the business model will generate a profit. The fundamental question is, Will enough customers be willing to pay for your product or service at a price that will cover your costs to produce or deliver the product or service and also fund your overhead and still leave a profit? The entrepreneur must understand how and when the business will generate revenues, and how much money is needed to sustain operations through breakeven. Many entrepreneurs think they can start a business and within one or two months begin generating revenue. This is rarely the case. The following are tools to help entrepreneurs become more objective when thinking about the economics of the business.

PRICING

Entrepreneurs must be objective when it comes to pricing their products or services. Because there is a lot at stake here, I have seen many entrepreneurs get caught up in fear-based thoughts: What if they won't be willing to pay enough for me to make money? What if I have to go back to the manufacturer and negotiate lower product costs and the manufacture is not willing? I love the packaging right now, it really makes the product, but what if I have to look at cheaper packaging?

For obvious reasons there seems to be a lot of angst about this. It seems at this point of discovering the business model, it is no longer about discovery: it is about making money. The bottom line is that entrepreneurs tend to make assumptions about pricing. It is not enough to compare the prices of competitors and price your product lower. It is not enough to use a mathematical model to determine what is needed to break even and then assume customers will pay that amount. The entrepreneur must determine how much the primary target customer is willing to pay for the product or service based on its unique value proposition. Again, the only way to do this is to talk to more customers. Some entrepreneurs have used customer surveys to get feedback on various pricing models, but they have found that it is not a real test. Sometimes even surveys may not be objective enough, because there is often a gap between what people *say* they will pay for a product and what they will *actually* pay for a product at the point of purchase. Hopefully by now, the entrepreneur loves talking to customers and will be happy to go back out and conduct more customer interviews with the MVP. As we reviewed earlier, it is important to identify your preferences, your assumptions, and your expectations first, then develop your hypothesis for testing. Again, once you are aware of your mental models, it is easier to be objective when designing your pricing test. It is important when developing your hypothesis to consider the normal inputs such as competitive pricing, the mathematical pricing model based on breakeven. You should also evaluate the strength of the previous responses to your MVP and the economic status of your core customer. Once you have developed a reasonable hypothesis to test, engage at least ten more customers across all of your customer segments and present them with three different price points; start with the highest to the lowest and watch their responses.

PROFITABILITY

As we discussed, understanding the profitability of the business model is key. To determine the viability of the business, the entrepreneur must forecast gross margin based on the price customers are willing to pay and how much it costs to produce the product. Gross margin equals revenues minus cost of goods sold. Entrepreneurs must be aware that this assessment can be misleading initially, and not a true picture of the financial viability of the business model long term. The challenge is that many entrepreneurs, when starting their businesses, need to produce limited quantities of products, yet the manufacturers have much higher minimum-order quantities. I have often seen entrepreneurs forced to pay significant premiums, perhaps 15 percent or more, to produce their product. Or if they have cash, they are forced to order the higher quantities and end up holding large quantities of inventory. Depending on the type of business, this can be a significant drain on financial resources. The most objective approach to this problem is to cultivate more than one manufacturing resource and understand the order quantity/cost breaks, but even then, the entrepreneur cannot know when demand will increase to justify the higher order quantities. I recommend calculating the gross margin based on the highest cost of goods, and if the business still looks profitable, I would consider it viable.

START-UP COSTS

Many entrepreneurs tend to underestimate what it will actually cost to set up operations for their businesses. The entrepreneur must go back to their Infrastructure and Resources Grid and discern the primary activities and related costs required to acquire customers and generate revenue. Some entrepreneurs require initial inventory; others require an e-commerce website. Some entrepreneurs will require office technology, while others will require other equipment. The best rule of thumb that we always say at Babson is to think cash last. If there are opportunities to get the resources you need without the outlay of cash, that is always best. An entrepreneur must be frugal and discerning when establishing initial operations. The key is to detail everything. Go back to your Infrastructure and Resources Grid and get actual quotes for every resource identified. For example, if it is an outside vendor, begin negotiation costs and payment terms. If it is a physical resource, negotiate with at least two to three suppliers to get the best price. If it is an employee, try to find comparable salaries for your industry. If you cannot afford to pay for the person at a reasonable salary, think creatively about offering equity or other incentives such as bonuses based on performance, et cetera. Whether it is a one-time purchase, a unit expense, or monthly expense, negotiate the lowest price and start building a start-up cost spreadsheet. The key here is to calculate how much money you will need to execute the scalable business model you have discovered.

OPERATING COSTS AND WORKING CAPITAL

This is critical. The entrepreneur must understand how much money is needed to sustain the business through breakeven. As we have learned, objectivity means dealing with "what is." When estimating working capi-tal needs, the entrepreneur does not know how long it will take to generate revenue. It is difficult to get objective data about the average length of time to breakeven for start-up companies. There are just so many variables. The best approach is to focus on your burn rate, which is your average monthly operating expenses. Again, go back to your Infrastructure and Resources Requirements Grid component and detail the monthly expenses you will need to incur to maintain your operations. This includes office expenses, salaries, marketing, et cetera. Once you have a sense of your burn rate, i.e., your monthly operating expense, you will be able to calculate your net profit, a key measure of financial viability. From a financial requirement perspective, given that you can only predict and not really know when you will be able to negotiate better manufacturing terms, or when you will break even, the best rule of thumb is to assume that you will need to cover your burn rate for a specified period of time, depending on your business model. Your financial requirements, how much money you need to raise to execute your business model, is your start-up costs plus your operating expense for a period of time.

Interestingly, the 2012 Global Entrepreneurship Monitor United States report concludes that more than "43% of Americans believed there were good opportunities for entrepreneurship in 2012. And 56% of adults believed they had the capabilities to start a business. But one third of those who saw opportunities were constrained by fear of failure."[6] I hope we can eliminate that constraint by dispelling some of the myths about the entrepreneurial process and illuminating many of the unproductive mental models that undermine entrepreneurs. Given the new knowledge you have about the entrepreneurial process and the objective approaches you have learned to manage it, perhaps more of you will leverage who you are, what you know, and who you know to discover an opportunity that is sustainable and that creates value for yourself and others.

Chapter 11

FINAL THOUGHTS: YOU AND THE POWER OF SEEING THINGS AS THEY ARE

I hope you have learned that your mind is more powerful than you probably ever imagined. You no longer have to be a victim of your thoughts, your moods, your current circumstances, or your past. At every moment, as the Subject, you can become aware of what you are thinking and how you are feeling and choose your perception of and response to everything you experience. How you perceive and experience the world is based on your mental models, your deeply held beliefs about yourself and the world. In this way, *your* world is in *your* mind! Just like all the other things about you that you did not choose—your gender, your skin color, your parents, et cetera—you also have the power to create your own reality, that is, your perception of, response to, and experience of the world. Instead of seeing and responding to the world through the lens of distorted mental models, you can leverage the power of seeing things as they are to create a better life. We all have this capacity.

Once you start this process and identify a mental model that is no longer valid and you see how it has impacted your life, there is often a feeling of joy. The joy comes from the realization that you no longer have to live your life through that lens, that you have the *power* to change it.

Learning to be objective is a journey of self-discovery—an ongoing process of self-awareness, moment-to-moment conscious effort, and self-reflection. So as you commit to the process of becoming a more objective leader, celebrate the little things, the small steps you are taking each day. Every time you respond more objectively, it will make a difference in your life. For example, if you are learning to be more mindful and present, celebrate every time you catch yourself creating mini-movies in your mind during a team meeting. Even if you can increase your mindfulness by only 5 percent in a day, you will be surprised how much more focused and productive you can be. Every time you choose not to believe that negative thought and don't allow it to spiral out of control you are improving you overall health and well-being. Each time you decide not to take something personally and instead deal with the issue at hand, you will improve your relationships with your coworkers. Every time you don't roll your eyes and judge someone for saying something that you think is stupid, you are fostering greater team collaboration. Greater objectivity yields greater results in all aspects of your life.

Conversely, if you find that after several private celebrations you overreact to something or judge someone's remark when you know you shouldn't, do not condemn yourself. It is absolutely critical that while you are in the process of transforming a mental model that you are kind to yourself. Remember that your old ways of responding have been hardwired and it takes time, patience, and focus to shift it. Every time you are impatient with yourself and disappointed in your response, you end up strengthening the old connection that you are trying to unwire. You can't be mad at your mind. Instead, have fun with it. When you find yourself doing what you normally do, just smile, acknowledge that it is the nature of the mind and that you will make the changes you desire in time. You are the Subject. You do have the power to change your mind! We can be so hard on ourselves, even when learning to be more objective. Instead of beating yourself up, view it as an opportunity to learn what your triggers are so you may avoid the response the next time. Remember, fatigue, deadline pressure, and other stresses can derail your ability to be objective in the moment. So when you know you are tired or stressed, try to be more vigilant and aware of your triggers so you don't respond in a way you will regret. Celebrate your responses when they are consistent with your objectives, and learn from the responses that are not.

And finally, do not underestimate the power of your beliefs about yourself and how much they influence everything in your life. While you are working on responding more objectively moment to moment, it is essential that you learn to be objective about yourself, which means seeing and accepting yourself as you are.

You are indeed more powerful than you think! You are only limited by what you believe about yourself. You are the Subject. If you believe and tell yourself that you can't achieve something, then you limit your ability to achieve it. It is a matter of belief. I urge you to identify and challenge your underlying assumptions about yourself and create new models that will help you reach your fullest potential. As Hillary Clinton said in her June 2014 town hall meeting on CNN: "What you think about yourself, what you say to others about yourself really does affect how you present yourself and eventually who you are."[1]

We all have the power to change our minds, to change our experience of the world, and to achieve our goals. And ultimately, together, we have the power to change the world. Never before has the need for greater objectivity been clearer as the consequences of our inherent subjectivity continue to play out on a global scale. Now, imagine what the world would be like if people of all walks of life learned to see and respond to things as they are. Because we are all connected and interrelated in ways that we don't always understand, the positive effects of many people responding more objectively and living happier, more successful lives could help solve many of the world's problems today.

It starts with you and I wish you well on your journey to discover the *power of seeing things as they are.*

NOTES

CHAPTER 2: UNDERSTANDING SUBJECTIVITY

1. Denis Brian, *The Voice of Genius: Conversations with Nobel Scientists and Other Luminaries* (New York: Perseus Books, 1995), 127.
2. Robert A. Burton, *On Being Certain: Believing That You Are Right Even When You Are Not* (New York: St. Martin's Press, 2008), 158–59.

CHAPTER 3: THE SUBJECT–OBJECT RELATIONSHIP: HOW WE RELATE TO THE WORLD

1. Hugh J. Foley and Margaret W. Matline, *Sensation and Perception* (Old Tappan, NJ: Pearson Higher Education, 2010), 6–7.
2. Ibid.
3. V. S. Ramachandran, *The Tell-Tale Brain, A Neuroscientist's Quest for What Makes Us Human* (New York: Norton, 2011), 14.
4. Shankar Vedantam, *The Hidden Brain* (New York: Spiegel and Grau, 2010), 19.
5. David Rock and Jeffrey Schwartz, "The Neuroscience of Leadership," *Strategy+Business* 42 (Summer 2006): 3.
6. Daniel G. Amen, *Change Your Brain, Change Your Life* (New York: Three Rivers Press, 1998), 111–13.
7. Vedantam, *Hidden Brain*, 19.
8. Amen, *Change Your Brain, Change Your Life*, 82.
9. Donald Hebb, *The Organization of Behavior* (New York: Wiley & Sons, 1949; Mahwah, NJ: Lawrence Erlbaum, 2002), 63. Citations refer to the Lawrence Erlbaum edition.

10. David Rock, "Managing with the Brain in Mind," *Strategy+Business* 56 (Autumn 2009): 7.

11. Homer H. Johnson, "Mental Models and Transformative Learning: The Key to Leadership Development?" *Human Resource Development Quarterly* 19, no.1 (Spring 2008): 86.

12. Ellen J. Langer, *Mindfulness* (Cambridge, MA: DaCapo Press, 1989), 19–41.

13. Ibid.

14. Ibid., 22.

15. Amen, *Change Your Brain, Change Your Life*, 56–57.

16. Byron Katie, *Loving What Is: Four Questions That Can Change Your Life* (New York: Three Rivers Press, 2002), 23–24.

17. Rick Hanson and Richard Mendius, *Buddha's Brain: The Practical Neuroscience of Happiness, Love and Wisdom* (Oakland, CA: New Harbinger, 2009), 41.

18. Rock and Schwartz, "Neuroscience of Leadership," 5.

19. Ibid., 4.

20. Neurophilosophy, *The Neurological Basis of Intuition*, February 9, 2009, http://scienceblogs.com/neurophilosophy/2009/02/09/the-neurological-basis-of-intuition/.

21. Science News Staff, "The Brains Behind Intuition," *Science,* February 28, 1997, http://news.sciencemag.org/1997/02/brains-behind-intuition.

22. Sharon Begley, *Train Your Mind, Change Your Brain* (New York: Ballantine Books, 2008).

CHAPTER 4: OBJECTIVE DECISION MAKING

1. Aaron T. Beck, *Cognitive Therapies and Emotional Disorders* (New York: New American Library, 1976).

2. Ibid.

3. Byron Katie, *Loving What Is: Four Questions That Can Change Your Life* (New York: Three Rivers Press, 2002), 23–4.

CHAPTER 5: OBJECTIVITY UNDER PRESSURE

1. Jon Kabat-Zinn, *Mindfulness for Beginners: Reclaiming the Present Moment—and Your Life* (Louisville, CO: Sounds True, 2012), 1.

2. Ibid.

3. Ellen J. Langer, *Mindfulness* (Cambridge, MA: DaCapo Press, 1989), 33–34.

4. Rick Hanson and Richard Mendius, *Buddha's Brain: The Practical Neuroscience of Happiness, Love and Wisdom* (Oakland, CA: New Harbinger, 2009), 44–45.

5. Kabat-Zinn, *Mindfulness for Beginners*, 148.

CHAPTER 6: CHANGING YOUR MIND: IDENTIFYING AND SHIFTING LIMITING MENTAL MODELS

1. Homer H. Johnson, "Mental Models and Transformative Learning: The Key to Leadership Development?" *Human Resource Development Quarterly* 19, no. 1 (Spring 2008), 86.

2. Charles Horton Cooley and Han-Joachim Schubert, *On Self and Social Organization* (Chicago: University of Chicago Press, 1998), 20.

3. Ellen J. Langer, *Mindfulness* (Cambridge, MA: DaCapo Press, 1989), 33–34.

4. Sharon Begley, *Train Your Mind, Change Your Brain* (New York: Ballantine Books, 2008), 194.

5. David Rock and Jeffrey Schwartz, "The Neuroscience of Leadership," *Strategy+Business* 42 (Summer 2006): 8.

6. Swamiji Dayananda Saraswati, *The Yoga Of Objectivity* (Chennai, India: Arsha Vidya Research and Publication Trust, 2010).

7. D. A. Bryant and N. U. Frigaard, "Prokaryotic Photosynthesis and Phototrophy Illuminated," *Trends in Microbiology* 14, no. 11 (November 2006): 488–96.

8. Ibid., 9.

CHAPTER 7: CREATING INCLUSIVE ENVIRONMENTS

1. Anderson Cooper and Soledad O'Brien, "Readers: Children Learn Attitudes about Race at Home," *Anderson Cooper 360*, CNN, May 25, 2010, http://www.cnn.com/2010/US/05/13/doll.study/.

2. Mahzarin R. Banaji and Anthony G. Greewald, *Blind Spot: Hidden Biases of Good People* (New York: Delacorte Press, 2013), 3–52.

3. Ibid.

4. Ibid., 70.

5. M. J. Margo Monteith and A. Y. Mark, "The Self-Regulation of Prejudice," in *Handbook of Stereotyping, Prejudice, and Discrimination*, ed. T. D. Nelson (New York: Psychology Press, 2009), 356.

CHAPTER 8: MANAGING TEAMS AND ORGANIZATIONAL CHANGE

1. Rob Enderle, "Lessons from Ballmer's Microsoft," *Datamation*, February 4, 1014, http://www.datamation.com/commentary/lessons-from-ballmers-microsoft.html.

2. Deidre L. Redmond, "A Black Female Professor Struggles with 'Going Mean,'" *Chronicle of Higher Education*, May 27, 2014, http://chronicle.com/article /A-Black-Female-Professor/146739/?cid=at&utm_source=at&utm_ medium=en.

3. Monica Langley, "Ballmer on Ballmer: His Exit from Microsoft," *Wall Street Journal*, November 17, 2013.

4. Ibid.

5. Ibid.

6. Ibid.

7. John P. Kotter, "Leading Change: Why Transformation Efforts Fail," *Harvard Business Review*, March 1995.

8. David Rock and Jeffrey Schwartz, "The Neuroscience of Leadership," *Strategy+Business* 42 (Summer 2006): 5.

9. Kotter, "Leading Change."

CHAPTER 9: THE OBJECTIVE LEADER AND THE ASPIRING ENTREPRENEUR

1. Saras D. Saraswathy, *Effectuation: Elements of Entrepreneurial Expertise* (Northhampton, MA: Edgar Elgar Publishing, 2008), 17.

2. Danna Greenberg, Kate McKone-Sweet, H. James Wilson, and Babson Faculty, *The New Entrepreneurial Leader* (San Francisco: Berrett-Koehler, 2011), 31.

3. Saraswathy, *Effectuation*, 17.

4. Ibid., 189.

5. Alexander Osterwalder and Yves Pigneur, *Business Model Generation* (Hoboken, NJ: John Wiley & Sons, 2012).

6. Jason Delrey, "The Art of the Pivot," *Inc. Magazine*, February 1, 2011.

7. Saraswathy, *Effectuation*, 73.

8. Candida Brush, Moriah Meyskens, Robert Nason, and Babson College, *The Global Entrepreneurship Monitor Massachusetts, 2010 Report*, 18. The Global Entrepreneurship Research Association (GERA) is, for formal constitutional and regulatory purposes, the umbrella organization that hosts the GEM project. GERA is an association formed of Babson College, London Business School, and representatives of the Association of GEM national

teams. http://www.babson.edu/Academics/centers/blank-center/global-research/gem/Documents/gem-2010-massachusetts-report.pdf.

9. Saraswathy, *Effectuation*, 81.

10. Fasal Hoque, "Why Most Venture Backed Companies Fail," *Fast Company*, December 10, 2012, http://www.fastcompany.com/3003827/why-most-venture-backed-companies-fail.

11. Jay Goltz, "Top 10 Reasons Small Businesses Fail," *New York Times*, January 5, 2011.

12. Donna J. Kelley, Abdul Ali, Edward J. Rogoff, Candida Brush, Andrew Corbett, Mahdi Majbouri, Diana Hechavarria, Babson College, and Baruch College, *Global Entrepreneurship Monitor 2012 United States Report*, 19, http://www.gemconsortium.org/docs/download/2804.

CHAPTER 10: THE OBJECTIVE ENTREPRENEUR'S BUSINESS MODEL MAP

1. Eric Ries, *The Lean Startup: How Today's Entrepreneurs Use Continuous Innovation to Create Radically Successful Businesses* (New York: Crown Business, 2011), 22.

2. Alexander Osterwalder and Yves Pigneur, *The Business Model Generation* (Edison, NJ: John Wiley & Sons, 2010), 15.

3. Steve Blank, "Why the Lean Start-Up Changes Everything," *Harvard Business Review*, May 2013, 5.

4. Steve Blank and Bob Dorf, "How to Test Your Minimum Viable Product," *Inc. Magazine*, June 12, 2012, 2.

5. Dan Newman, "How to Sell to the Hyper-Aware Consumer," *Entrepreneur Magazine*, March 27.

6. Donna J. Kelley, Abdul Ali, Candida Brush, Andrew C. Corbett, Mahdi Majbouri, Edward G. Rogoff, Babson College, and Baruch College, *Global Entrepreneurship Monitor 2012 United States Report*, 6.

CHAPTER 11: FINAL THOUGHTS: YOU AND THE POWER OF SEEING THINGS AS THEY ARE

1. CNN Town Hall, "Hillary Clinton's Hard Choices," June 17, 2014, transcript, accessed September 5, 2014, http://transcripts.cnn.com/TRANSCRIPTS/1406/17/se.01.html.

INDEX